P9-CQG-888

I have given thee the power of flight without wings

EQUUS REINED

ROBERT VAVRA

William Morrow and Company, Inc.

New York

For Hector and Karen who represent all that is noble in the relationship of horse and man

Copyright © 1987 by Robert Vavra

All rights reserved. No part of this book may be reproduced or utilized in any form or by any means, electronic or mechanical, including photocopying, recording or by any information storage and retrieval system, without permission in writing from the Publisher. Inquiries should be addressed to Permissions Department, William Morrow and Company, Inc., 105 Madison Ave., New York, N.Y. 10016.

Library of Congress Cataloging-in-Publication Data

Vavra, Robert.
  Equus reined.
    1. Horses—Pictorial works. I. Title.
SF303.V378   1987   636.1   87-13911
ISBN 0-688-05089-1

Printed in Spain by Cayfosa, Barcelona. Dep. Leg. B-27503-1987

1 2 3 4 5 6 7 8 9 10

Book design by the Author

Drawings by John Fulton

REFLECTIONS

I can't remember ever not loving horses. It's as though I was born infatuated with how they look, feel, smell, and sound. My father loved to tell us of his childhood in the American West; of having his small boy's eyes dazzled by the first electric light bulb turned on to illuminate the dusty streets of Cheyenne, Wyoming; of waiting in front of a saloon for a cowboy to ride up and say, "Hey, kid, hold my horse and I'll give you a nickel"; or of watching the overland stage pull into town, its team of horses lathered white under the load of exotic cargo and passengers brought to Cheyenne from "the outside world." He told of Indians coming into town to sell blankets and of Uncle John, his saddle-maker uncle, weaving out of saloons and along the wooden sidewalks after having been paid for one of the saddles that were fine enough to take him eventually to Hollywood where he would be employed by Gene Autry and Tom Mix. All of those precious memories from my father's treasure chest of experience were in some way related to horses and to the men who depended upon them.

My father's favorite story was about the outlaw Tom Horn. In the war between the cattlemen and the sheepmen, Horn had been contracted to gun down a sheep farmer and, in doing so, he mistakenly shot the teenage son of his intended victim. It was a famous court case with Horn counting on the support of the wealthy cattle ranchers to spring him from jail. My father told of walking the streets of Cheyenne with some other boys shortly before Horn was to have been hanged and of noticing several saddled, riderless horses tied and spaced leading out of town, one of which was tethered to the schoolhouse hitching post.

"Let's play Tom Horn making his escape!" said my father to his friends, who for the next half hour ran around the rickety building, using their hands as imaginary guns while shouting "Bang! Bang!" and "You're dead!" At one point in the game my father took the role of the hired killer and, as he sought a hiding place under the schoolhouse steps, discovered a neatly wrapped package that had been carefully wedged under one of the staircase's wooden supports. Removing the parcel from its hiding place, my father carefully untied the string and unfolded the newspaper to disclose two pearl-handled Colt .45 pistols. Just then his older brother Frank appeared, re-wrapped the guns, and ran off to show them to their Uncle Adolph. What happened to those pearl-handled Colt forty-fives, my father didn't know. Later, however, as a man, he deduced that the horses tied on the road out of town and the pistols under the schoolhouse steps had been carefully placed there for Tom Horn's jail break. And it is here that can be seen the importance of the horse in the world just a single generation ago.

(Continued on page 131)

Equus reineD

When God created the earth, the horse's destiny was an Eden of marshes and swamps—a paradise of fragrance, sound and color—inhabited by the most exotic of plants and creatures.

However, here all was not peaceful. Mares and foals were preyed upon by saber-toothed tigers and other mighty hunters, including man who in the eye of a herd stallion aroused both fear and anger.

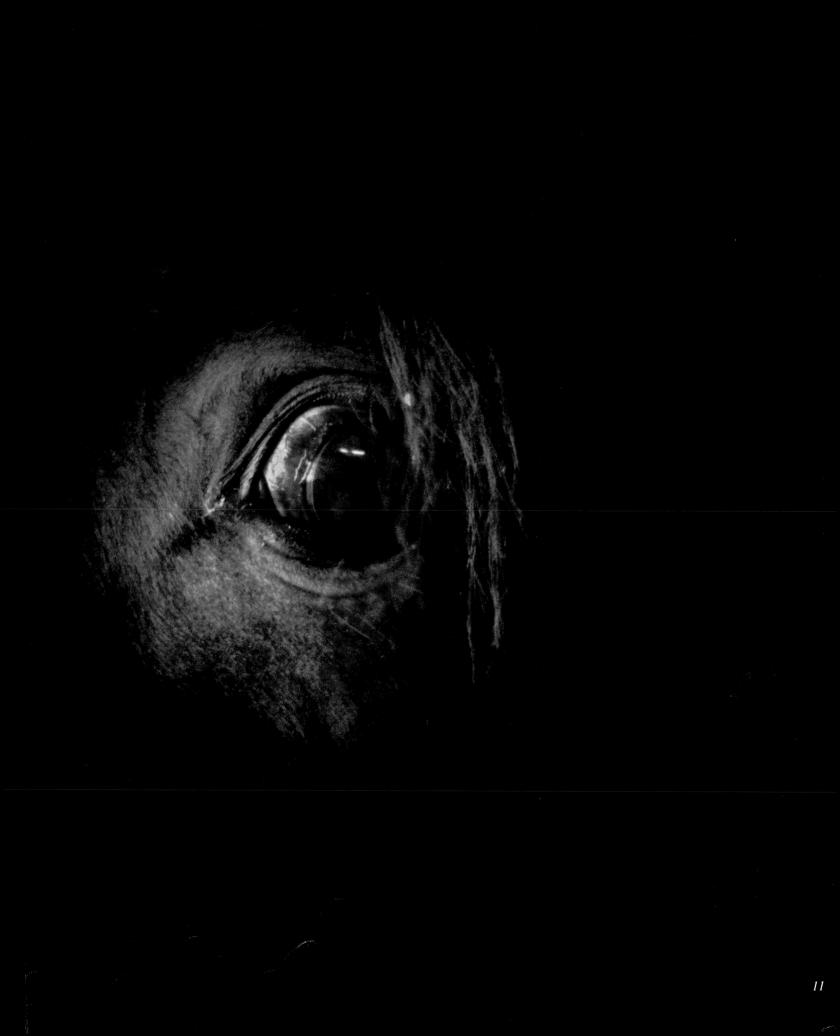

As he grew in size and evolved from an eater of leaves to one of grass, the horse's legs became tall and strong enough to carry him out of the low wetlands and onto the steppes. Here, his new speed allowed him to survive in a world of predators, among the most savage and dangerous of which was man.

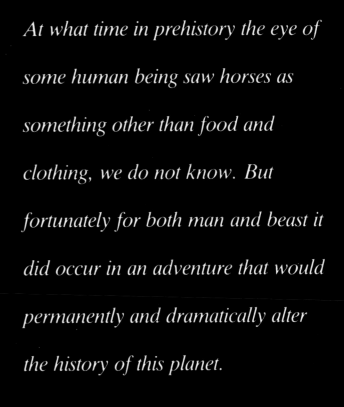

At what time in prehistory the eye of some human being saw horses as something other than food and clothing, we do not know. But fortunately for both man and beast it did occur in an adventure that would permanently and dramatically alter the history of this planet.

The youth's eyes were then on the filly foal and on it alone. With her capture the story of mankind would change in an instant and forever.

Trajan Tennent

. . . he . . . crouched low and watched the herd through a screen of tall, golden-green grass. . . . His attention was focused on a stallion . . . uncannily aware of impending danger to his harem.

Jean M. Auel

She loved . . . his touch, his caresses. She loved to have

his hands . . . all over her head and neck, smoothing

the silken softness of her skin, patting the sensitive

curves of her face . . . her forelock.

Mary O'Hara

Why did this animal that had prospered so in Colorado desert

his amiable homeland for Siberia? There is no answer. We

know that when the horse negotiated the land bridge . . . he

found on the other end opportunity for varied development that

is one of the bright aspects of animal history. He wandered into

France and became the mighty Percheron, and into Arabia,

where he developed into a lovely poem of a horse, and into

Africa, where he became the brilliant zebra, and into Scotland,

Look, what a horse should have he did not lack,

Save a proud rider on his back.

William Shakespeare

25

We be of one blood, ye and I . . .

Rudyard Kipling

The back of thy horse subjects the world

to thee.

I will fashion it into a throne for thee:

whence thou shalt wield a scepter of

power and joy and freedom, such as beyond

expectation.

Rudolf C. Binding

Wherever man has left his footprint

in the long ascent from barbarism to

civilization we will find the hoofprint

of the horse beside it.

John Trotwood Moore

After that I was driven every day for a week

or so, and as I appeared to be quite safe . . .

it was decided to keep me and call me by my

old name of "Black Beauty."

Anna Sewell

Horses of Africa,

African horses

exotic and brilliant

striped

with ebony

and

the snows of Kilimanjaro.

Traian Tennent

What is the passing strange force . . . in these passing strange steeds?

Steeds, steeds, what steeds!

Has the whirlwind a home in your manes?

. . . all things on earth fly by . . .

Nikolai Gogol

Some glory in their birth . . .

Some in their wealth,

some in their body's force.

Some in their hounds and hawks,

some in their horse.

William Shakespeare

Ride a cockhorse to Banbury Cross,

To see a fine lady upon a white horse;

Rings on her fingers and bells on her toes,

She shall have music wherever she goes.

Anonymous

My hand forever in your mane

so dense,

Rubies and pearls and sapphires

there will sow . . .

Oasis of my dreams, and gourd

from whence

Deep drafted wines of memory

will flow.

Charles Baudelaire

Look for me by moonlight;

Watch for me by moonlight;

I'll come to thee by moonlight,

though hell should bar the way!

Alfred Noyes

44

My beautiful, my beautiful! that standest meekly by,

With thy proudly-arched and glossy neck, and dark and fiery eye!

Fret not to roam the desert now, with all thy winged speed:

I may not mount on thee again!—thou'rt sold, my Arab steed!

Caroline E.S. Norton

I wish I could run like you, she thought. I wonder if I

wouldn't be happier if I were a horse instead of a

She lifted the drooping muzzle with both

hands . . . It was a special embrace saved for

special occasions.

Jean M. Auel

God forbid that I should go

to any heaven in which there

are no horses.

R. B. Cunninghame-Graham

Heaven is high, and earth wide. If you rise three feet higher above the ground than other men, you will know what that means.

Rudolf G. Binding

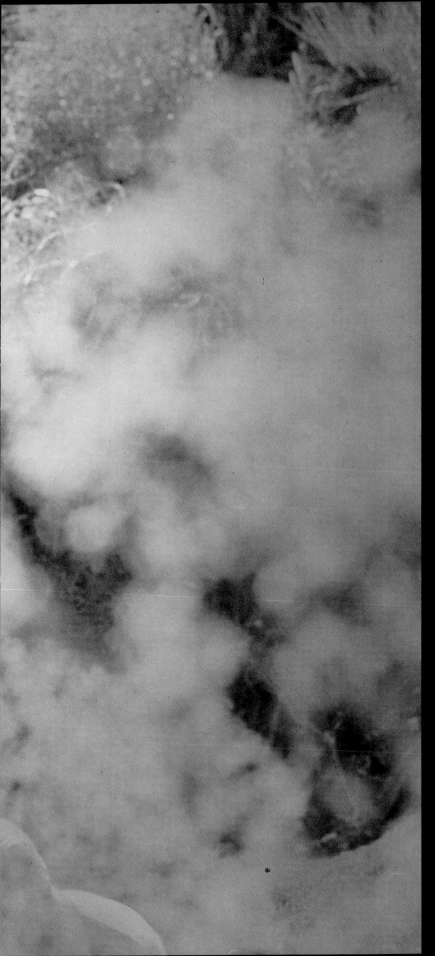

Who doth not feel, until his failing sight

Faints into dimness with its own delight,

His changing cheek, his sinking heart confess,

The might—the majesty of Loveliness.

Lord Byron

My horse be swift in flight.

Even like a bird;

My horse be swift in flight.

Bear me now in safety.

Far from the enemy arrows,

And you shall be rewarded

With streamers and ribbons red.

Sioux warrior's song to his horse

My horse has a hoof of striped agate,

His fetlock is like fine eagle plume

His legs are like quick lightning

My horse has a tail like a trailing black cloud.

His mane is made of short rainbows.

My horse's eyes are made of big stars

Navajo war god's horse song

. . . *he did not feel the ground under his*

feet . . . he thrust himself into the capriole,

rose high in the air . . . forelegs and hindlegs

horizontal. He soared above the ground, his

head high in jubilation. Conquering!

Felix Salten

To see her is to love her,

And love but her for ever,

For Nature made her what she is.

Robert Burns

"They're off!"

It seemed like a river of satin,

with iridescent foam pouring

against all nature . . . horses

grouped together . . . like some

theatrical illusion, as if a boat

going across a stage . . . I could

see the favorite going along like

some bird flying low . . . his

jockey hunched on his withers.

Donn Byrne

Sometimes he scuds farr off, and there he stares;

With gentle majesty and modest pride . . .

. . . he is pure air and fire; and the dull elements

of earth and water never appear in him . . .

He looks upon his love, and neighs unto her;

She answers him as if she knew his mind.

William Shakespeare

My horse the dolphin of the plain . . .

My boat of roses, steed of fire

At once the courser and the shallop,

The dolphin on whose surge I gallop . . .

Roy Campbell

This is the attitude used by artists

to depict the horses on which

gods and heroes ride.

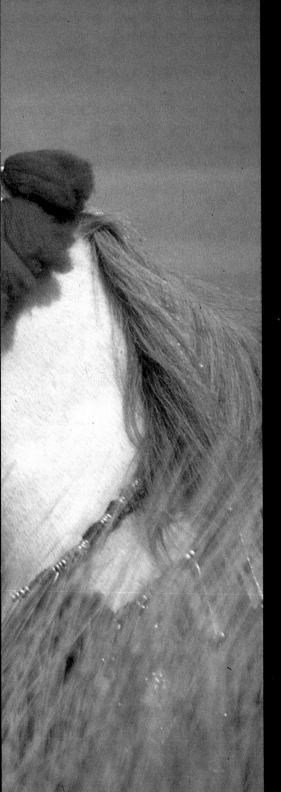

All the treasures of this earth lie between thine

eyes. Thou shalt cast Mine enemies beneath

thy hooves. . . . This shall be the seat from

whence prayers rise unto me.

The Koran

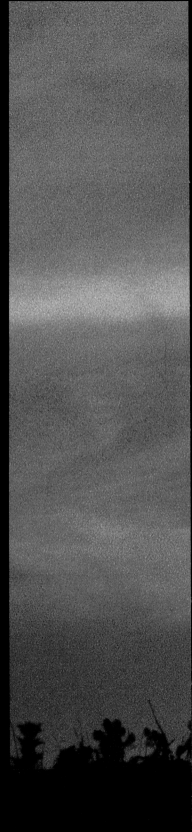

Away, away, my steed and I,

Upon the pinions of the wind,

We sped like meteors through the sky,

When with its crackily sound the night

Is chequer'd with the northern light.

Last night I passed at the edge

    of darkness,

And slept with green dew, alone.

I have come a long way, to

    surrender my shadow

To the shadow of my horse.

James Wright

The horse is a creature who sacrifices his own being to exist through the

will of another. . . . he is the noblest conquest of man.

Buffon

The trumpets sounded . . . the lances of the champions were lowered . . . the

Norman spurred against the Dis-inherited Knight. The two riders rushed against

each other in full gallop. . . . Nothing could have saved him except the remarkable strength of the noble horse.

Sir Walter Scott

The spear was used though death was not the

mission of this hunt. . . . Life was what he sought

. . . . then the foal was against his chest, heart

pounding against heart like counterpoint drums in

the African night.

Trajan Tennent

. . . Nature made her: beauty cost her nothing,

Her virtues were so rare.

George Chapman

Harnessed with the level rays in golden reins. . . . The sunlight, zithering their flanks

86   *with fire. . . .*

Flashes between the shadows as they pass. . . . Like wind along the golden strings

of a lyre.

Roy Campbell

Oh how in fury foaming at the rein

With coal red eye and cataracting mane . . .

Who shod the flying thunders on their feet

And plumed them with the snortings

of the sea . . .

Surely the great white breakers gave

them birth.

Roy Campbell

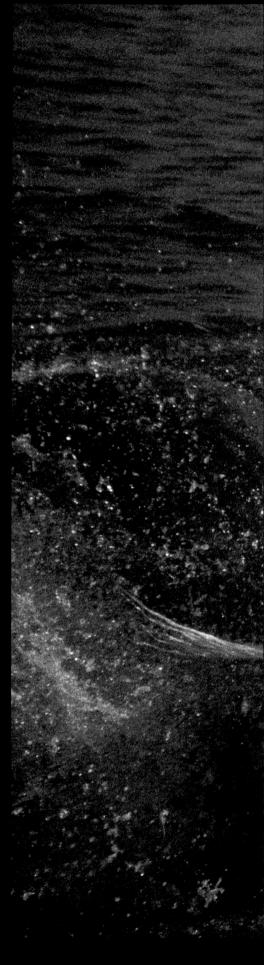

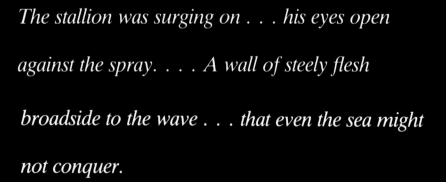

The stallion was surging on . . . his eyes open

against the spray. . . . A wall of steely flesh

broadside to the wave . . . that even the sea might

not conquer.

Charles Tenny Jackson

Nothing can bring back the hour

Of splendor in the grass, of glory in the flower.

William Wordsworth

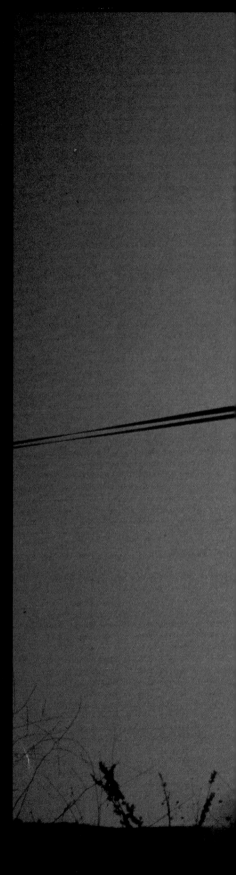

From the prick of his ears to the flow of his tail

he arched in my throat and eyes . . .

Oh, marvelous with the drifting clouds

he drifted across the skies!

William Rose Benét

94

A large white stallion . . . peered at me

oddly for several moments and then slowly

stretched his nose to mine. . . . His huge

eyes were like fishbowls holding exotic

creatures of serpentine colors.

Lynn V. Andrews

Where in the wide world can man find nobility without pride,

friendship without envy, or beauty without vanity? Here, where

grace is laced with muscle and strength by gentleness confined.

Ronald Duncan

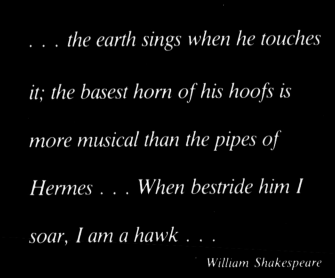

. . . the earth sings when he touches

it; the basest horn of his hoofs is

more musical than the pipes of

Hermes . . . When bestride him I

soar, I am a hawk . . .

William Shakespeare

The Angel that presided o'er

my birth

Said, "Little creature, form'd

of joy and mirth,

Go, love, without the help

of any thing on earth."

William Blake

Hoof patterns in the sand,

here

now,

gone

now.

. . . I heard a neigh, Oh such a

brisk and melodious neigh it was.

My very heart leaped with the

sound.

Nathaniel Hawthorne

. . . the floss-silk manes tossed up like

the crest of a breaking wave. . . . Light

ran and glittered on them. They were

obedient . . . you would have sworn

. . . as the white horses of the wave

crests are to the pull of the moon.

Mary Stewart

As the days went by Bucephalus grew to love the

boy Alexander more and more. They understood

each other, these two. They were friends.

Alice Gall and Fleming Crew

And forever streaming before me, fanning my forehead

cool,

Flowed a mane of molten silver,

and just before my thighs . . .

The steady pulse of those pinions,

their wonderful fall and rise!

William Rose Benét

I call my fastest horse from

darkness

horse that whispers,

horse patient as stone,

horse wild as wolf teeth.

Yaaaaaahhh!

Philip Daughtry

A wild . . . little Horse of Magic

came cantering out of the sky

With a bridle of silver and

into the saddle I mounted

To fly—and to fly.

Walter de la Mare

Surely she knew that he loved her and

was there just to serve and care for her,

and still, when he came near, there was

that alert turn of her head, the wary

look in her eye.

Mary O'Hara

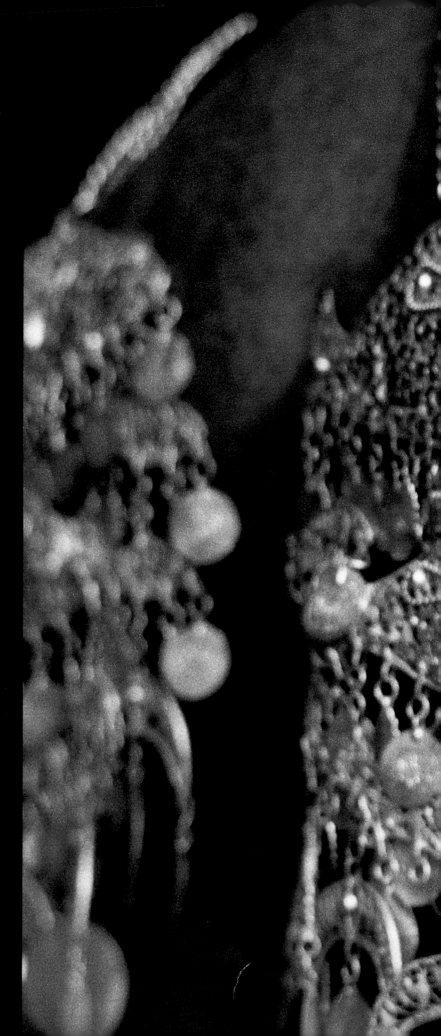

. . . we stretched . . . into the air,

fleeting on in the sunshine

a speck in the gleam

On galloping hoofs, his mane

in the wind out-flowing

As if in a dream.

Walter de la Mare

I have never seen such a perfectly formed animal.

Beautiful and graceful like a gazelle, he burned hot and

wild with the deserts of Egypt in his soul.

Lynn V. Andrews

To see a world in a grain of sand

And a heaven in a wild flower,

Hold infinity in the palm of your hand

And eternity in an hour.

William Blake

A horse! a horse! my kingdom for a horse!

William Shakespeare

Reflections Continued, and a Comment on the Photographs

(Continued from page 6)

Today, when cowboys roar into Cheyenne on payday, they screech over-size pickup trucks to a halt and drop quarters into parking meters before going into bars. In my father's day, they galloped into town on horses and gave a coin to a small child who held their live transportation at the swinging doors of rowdy saloons in front of which Indians sold their wares. Now, when visitors come to Cheyenne, they arrive in jet aircraft or air-conditioned motor vehicles, and their dress does not distinguish them from the locals. In my father's time, they could only arrive by horseback or in horse-drawn carriages and wagons from which they disembarked among the town's inhabitants like a cageful of exotic tropical birds set free in a farmyard. Now, when a criminal tries to break out of jail, he might use a helicopter, hand grenades, and a submachine gun. Then, Tom Horn staked his life on a string of cow ponies and a pair of pearl-handled Colt .45s hidden under the rickety steps of a schoolhouse.

We forget just what a short time ago it was—barely yesterday—that man depended so totally on equines. Today, with the exception of the cattle horse, equines in America and most of the world are luxury items—used only for show, sport, and pleasure. They are dispensable.

History, however, testifies that man's association with horses exemplifies, perhaps, the most profound animal-human relationship in recorded experience. While dogs are said to be our "best friends," still the animal names etched in human history are those of horses: Bucephalus, Rosinante, Morengo, and Babieca. This fascination with equines is also illustrated by the abundance of horses in literature: Black Beauty, Flicka, Thunderhead, the Black Stallion, Smoky.

However, at the dawn of time, the equine-human relationship was not one of friendship and romance. Then, man was a savage beast who, if he existed in that ape-like form today, would be behind bars in a zoo. And the horse of prehistory was a creature so small and devoid of physical beauty that if he were put on exhibit today, few passersby would stop to give him a second look.

The story of how that seemingly insignificant creature evolved into the animal that would provide the most opulent of thrones for kings and the most desired battle seat for generals—about which sonnets would be written—is one of the most fascinating sagas in animal evolution. And mine was the good fortune to have a master story-teller relate it to me.

Some years ago, James A. Michener, with whom I did the book *Iberia*, and I were together in California when movie director-turned-equestrian Budd Boetticher invited us to spend the night with him and his wife Mary at their home near Ramona. After directing the Carlos Arruza film, Budd had become fascinated with *rejoneo*, or bullfighting from horseback. Spanish and Portuguese *rejoneadors*, or gentlemen mounted bullfighters, are not to be confused with the unpopular picadors of the corrida. While mounted on highly   *131*

trained and valuable horses, the *rejoneador* plays the bull, whose horns are generally blunted or encased in leather sheaths and seldom touch the elegant stallions and mares that glide before them.

Budd Boetticher had constructed a small bullring near the equestrian center where he stables his horses, and on that cold fall afternoon he and Mary gave a special performance of Iberian horsemanship at which Michener was the honored guest. As we sat in the bleachers, *pasadoble* music blasting our ears while Budd and his stallion charged across the sand pursued by a pair of bull horns mounted with metal struts on a bicycle wheel that was pushed violently by a chunky, blond ex-football player, I felt as though I were part of some surrealistic Dali dream, rather than of the reality of that chilly gray afternoon in Ramona, California.

At the conclusion of the performance, Budd and Mary Boetticher hosted a party for Michener which was attended by a crowd of Hollywood personalities and land developers, as well as simple, local, country folk. For me it was a special gathering—among the guests were two of my childhood heroes: muscleman former movie star Steve Reeves and rodeo celebrity Casey Tibbs—and, except for the money talk of the land developers, conversation was mostly about what we all loved best—horses.

The following morning, before Budd drove us to the San Diego airport, he took Jim Michener to the stable to say good-bye to the stallions.

Michener has a special feeling for all life, a sensitivity that I had seen him display with fireflies and dogs at his home in Bucks County, with a parrot, a mongoose, and a hyena in Spain, and with a cat and pigeons in Portugal. Budd's stallions sensed this compassion and within seconds were nuzzling Jim's face. It was a delightful moment, to see two such noble beings seemingly entranced with each other's company.

From San Diego, Michener and I flew to Denver where, upon arriving at the airport, he said, "Let's drop the bags at the hotel, there's something I want to show you, and if we don't go right now, there won't be time."

The Denver Museum of Natural History is an impressive building, but then most natural history collections are housed in similarly vast structures. Years before, my excitement would always mount to a peak whenever my parents took us to the Los Angeles County Museum. It was a forever-fascinating voyage from the outside reality and sunlight into the darkness of the museum interior where dioramas and displays swept imagination back through time and across oceans and to jungles and places that before had existed only in dreams.

Then, as James Michener and I stood in the blackness of the great hall, he said, "Well, Robert, see that little creature. That's your equus." And for the next hour, he led me from display to display tracing through time the development of the animal that had left never-to-be-erased hoofprints on my childhood and which was then still looming

with the same importance on the horizon of my adult being. As people around us spoke in whispers and animals seemed transfixed in time behind the glass barriers, Jim told the story of equus in words not unlike those that he had used in his novel *Centennial*:

"Fifty-three million years ago, while the New Rockies were still developing and long after diplodocus had vanished, in the plains area, where the twin pillars formed, an animal began to develop which in later times would give man his greatest assistance, pleasure and mobility. The progenitor of this invaluable beast was a curious little creature, a four-legged mammal, for the age of reptiles was past, and he stood only seven or eight inches high at the shoulder. He weighed little, had a body covering of part-fur, part-hair and seemed destined to develop into nothing more than a small inconsequential beast.

"He had, however, three characteristics which would determine his future potential. The bones in his four short legs were complete and separate and capable of elongation. On each foot he had five small toes, that mysteriously perfect number which had characterized most of the ancient animals, including the great dinosaurs. And he had forty-four teeth, arranged in an unprecedented manner: in front, some peglike teeth as weak as those of diplodocus; then a conspicuous open space; then at the back of the jaw, numerous grinding molars.

"This little animal made no impression on his

age, for he was surrounded by other much larger mammals destined for careers as rhinoceroses, camels and sloths. He lived carefully in the shady parts of such woods as had developed and fed himself by browsing on leaves and soft marsh plants, for his teeth were not strong and would quickly have worn down had they been required to eat rough food like the grass which was even then beginning to develop.

"If one had observed all the mammals of this period and tried to evaluate the chances of each to amount to something, one would not have placed this quiet little creature high on the list of significant progenitors; indeed, it seemed then like an indecisive beast which might develop in a number of different ways, none of them memorable, and it would have occasioned no surprise if the little fellow had survived a few million years and then quietly vanished. Its chances were not good.

"The curious thing about this little forerunner of greatness is that although we are sure that he existed and are intellectually convinced that he had to have certain characteristics, no man has ever seen a shred of physical evidence that he really did exist. No fossil bone of this little creature has so far been found; we have tons of bones of diplodocus and her fellow reptiles, all of whom vanished, but of this small prototype of one of the great animal families, we have no memorials whatever. Indeed, he has not yet even been named, although we are quite familiar with his attributes; perhaps when his bones are ultimately found— 133

and they will be—a proper name would be 'paleohippus,' the hippus of the Paleocene epoch. When word of his discovery is flashed around the world, scholars and laymen in all countries will be delighted, for they will have come into contact with the father of a most distinguished race, one which all men have loved and from which most have profited.

"Perhaps thirteen million years after 'paleohippus' flourished, and when the land that would contain the twin pillars had begun to form, the second in line and first-known in this animal family appeared and became so numerous that in the land about the future pillars hundreds of skeletons would ultimately be laid down in rock, so that scientists would know this small creature as familiarly as they know their own puppies.

"He was eohippus, an attractive small animal about twelve inches high at the shoulder. He looked more like a friendly dog than anything else, with small alert ears, a swishing tail to keep insects away, a furry kind of coat and a longish face, which was needed to accommodate the forty-four teeth, which persisted. The teeth were still weak, so that the little creature had to content himself with leaves and other soft foods.

"But the thing that marked eohippus and made one suspect that this family of animals might be headed in some important direction was the feet. On the short front feet, not yet adapted for swift movement, the five original toes had been reduced to four; one had only recently disappeared,

the bones which had once sustained it vanishing into the leg. And on the rear foot there were now three toes, the two others having withered away during the course of evolution. But the surviving toes had tiny hoofs instead of claws.

"One could still not predict what this inconspicuous animal was going to become, and the fact that he would stand second in the sixty-million-year process of creating a noble animal seemed unlikely. Eohippus seemed more suited for a family pet than for an animal of distinction and utility.

"And then, about thirty million years ago, when the land that was to form the twin pillars was being laid down, mesohippus developed, twenty-four inches high at the shoulders and with all the basic characteristics of his ancestors, except that he had only three toes on each of his feet. He was a sleek animal, about the size of our collie or red fox. The forty-four teeth kept his face long and lean and his legs were beginning to lengthen, but his feet still contained pads and small hoofs.

"Then, about eighteen million years ago, a dramatic development took place which solved the mystery. Merychippus appeared, a most handsome three-toed animal forty inches high, with bristly mane, extended face and protective bars behind the eye sockets.

"He had one additional development which would enable the horse family to survive in a changing world: his teeth acquired the remarkable capacity to grow out from the socket as they wore down at the crown. This permitted the proto-horse to quit browsing on such leaves as he found and to move instead to grazing on the new grasses that were developing on the prairies. For grass is a dangerous and difficult food; it contains silica and other roughnesses that wear down teeth, which must do much grinding in order to prepare the grass for digestion. Had not merychippus developed these self-renewing grinders, the horse as we know it could have neither developed nor survived. But with this almost magical equipment, he was prepared.

"These profound evolutions occurred on the plains that surrounded the site of the twin pillars. There on flat lands that knew varied climates, from tropical to sub-arctic, depending upon where the equator was located at the time, this singular breed of animal went through the manifold changes that were necessary before it stood forth as an accomplished horse.

"One of the biggest changes in the antecedents of the horse appeared about six million years ago, when pliohippus, the latest in the breed, evolved with only one toe on each foot and with the pads on which his ancestors had run eliminated. It now had a single hoof. This animal was a medium-sized beautiful horse in almost every sense of the word, and would have been recognized as such, even from a considerable distance. There would be minor refinements, mostly in the teeth and in the shape of the skull, but the horse of historic times was now foreshadowed.

"He arrived as equus about two million years ago, as splendid an animal as the ages were to produce. Starting from the mysterious and unseen 'paleohippus,' this breed had unconsciously and with great persistence adapted itself to all the changes that the earth presented, adhering always to those mutations which showed the best chance of future development. 'Paleohippus,' of the many capacities, eohippus of the subtle form, merychippus with the horselike appearance, pliohippus with the single hoof—these attributes persisted; there were dozens of other variations equally interesting which died out because they did not contribute to the final form. There were would-be horses of every description, some with the most ingenious novelties, but they did not survive, for they failed to adjust to the earth as it was developing; they vanished because they were not needed. But the horse, with its notable collection of virtues and adjustments, did survive.

"About one million years ago, when the twin pillars were well formed, a male horse with chestnut coloring and flowing tail lived in the area as part of a herd of about ninety. He was three years old and gifted with especially strong legs that enabled him to run away more swiftly than most of his fellows. He was a gamin creature and had left his mother sooner than any of the other males of his generation. He was the first to explore new arrivals on the prairie and had developed the bad habit of leading any horses that would follow on excursions into canyons or along extended draws. 135

One bright summer morning this chestnut was leading a group of six adventurous companions on a short foray from the main herd. He took them across the plains that reached out from the twin pillars and northward into a series of foothills that contained passageways down which they galloped in file, their tails flowing free behind them as they ran. It was an exhilarating chase, and at the end of the main defile they turned eastward toward a plain that opened out invitingly, but as they galloped they saw blocking their way two mammoths of extraordinary size. The great smooth-skinned creatures towered over the horses, for they were gigantic, fourteen feet tall at the shoulders, with monstrous white tusks that curved downward from the head. The tips of the tusks reached sixteen feet, and if they caught an adversary, they could toss him far into the air. The two mammoths were imposing creatures, and had they been ill-disposed toward the horses, could have created havoc, but they were placid by nature, intending no harm.

"The chestnut halted his troop, led them at a sober pace around the mammoths, coming very close to the great tusks, then broke into a gallop which would take him onto the eastern plains, where a small herd of camels grazed, bending awkwardly forward. The horses ignored them, for ahead stood a group of antelope as if waiting for a challenge. The seven horses passed at full speed, whereupon the fleet antelope, each with a crown of four large antlers, sprang into action, darting after them.

For a few moments the two groups of animals were locked in an exciting race, the horses a little in the lead, but with a burst of speed the antelopes leaped ahead and before long the horses saw only dust. It had been a joyous race, to no purpose other than the challenge of testing speed.

"Beside the grazing area on which the antelope had been feeding there rested a family of armadillos, large ratlike creatures encased in collapsible armor. The horses were vaguely aware of them but remained unconcerned, for the armadillo was a slow, peaceful creature that caused no harm. But now the round little animals stopped searching for slugs and suddenly rolled themselves into a defensive position. Some enemy, unseen to the horses, was approaching from the south and in a moment it appeared, a pack of nine dire wolves, the scourge of the plains, with long fangs and swift legs. They loped easily over the hill that marked the horizon, peering this way and that, sniffing at the air. The wolf serving as scout detected the armadillos and signaled his mates. The predators hurried up, inspected the armor-plated round balls, nudged them with their noses and turned away. No food there.

"With some apprehension, the horses watched the nine enemies cross the grassland, hoping that they would pass well to the east, but this was not to be. The lead wolf, a splendid beast with sleek gray coat, spotted the horses and broke into a powerful run, followed instantly by his eight hunting companions. The chestnut snorted and in the flash of a moment realized that he must not lead his six

136 after them.

horses back into the canyon from which they had just emerged, for the two mammoths might block the way, allowing the dire wolves to overtake any straggler and cut him down.

"So with an adroit leap sideways he broke onto the plains in the direction the antelope had taken and led his troop well away from their home terrain. They galloped with purpose, for although the dire wolves were not yet close at hand, they had anticipated the direction the horses might take and had vectored to the east to cut them off. The chestnut, seeing this maneuver, led his horses to the north, which opened a considerable space between them and the wolves.

"As they ran to their own safety, they passed a herd of camels that were slower-moving. The big awkward beasts saw the apprehension of the horses and took fright, although what the cause of the danger was they did not yet know. There was a clutter on the prairie and much dust, and when it had somewhat settled, the horses were well on their way to safety but the camels were left in the direct path of the wolves. The lumbering camels ran as fast as they could, scattering to divert attack, but this merely served to identify the slowest-moving and upon this unfortunate the wolves concentrated.

"Cutting at him from all sides with fearful teeth, the wolves began to wear him down. He slowed. His head drooped. He had no defense against the dire wolves and within a few moments one had leaped at his exposed throat. Another fastened onto his right flank and a third slashed at his belly. Uttering a futile cry of anguish, the camel collapsed, his ungainly feet buckling under him, so that before the horses left the area, the camel had been slain.

"At a slow walk they headed south for the hills that separated them from the land of the twin pillars. On the way they passed a giant sloth who stood sniffing at the summer air, dimly aware that wolves were on the prowl. The huge beast, twice the size of the largest horse, knew from the appearance of the horses that they had encountered wolves, and retreated awkwardly to a protected area. An individual sloth, with his powerful fore-claws and hulking weight, was a match for one wolf, but if caught by a pack, he could be torn down, so battle was avoided.

"Now the chestnut led his horses into the low hills, down a gully and out onto the home plains. In the distance the twin pillars—white at the bottom where they stood on the prairie, reddish toward the top, and white again where the protecting caps rested—were reassuring, a signal of home, and when all seven of the troop were through the pass, they cantered easily back to the main herd. Their absence had been noted and various older horses came up to nuzzle them. The herd had a nice sense of community, as if all were members of the same family, and each was gratified when others who had been absent returned safely.

"Among the six followers accompanying the chestnut on his foray was a young dun-colored mare, and in recent weeks she had been keeping close to him and he to her. They obviously felt an association, a responsibility each to the other, and normally they would by now have bred, but they were inhibited by a peculiar awareness that soon they would be on the move. None of the older animals had signified in any way that the herd was about to depart this congenial land by the twin pillars, but in some strange way the horses knew that they were destined to move . . . and to the north.

"What was about to happen would constitute one of the major mysteries of the animal world. The horse, that splendid creature which had developed here at twin pillars, would desert his ancestral home and emigrate to Asia, where he would prosper, and the congenial plains at the pillars would be occupied by other animals. Then, about four hundred thousand years later, the horse would return from Asia to reclaim the pastures along the river, but by the year 6000 B.C. he would become extinct in the Western Hemisphere.

"The horses were about to move north and they knew they could not accommodate a lot of colts, so the chestnut and the mare held back, but one cold morning, when they had been chasing idly over the plains as if daring the dire wolves to attack them, they found themselves alone at the mouth of a canyon where the sun shone brightly, and he mounted her and in due course she produced a handsome colt.

"It was then that the herd started its slow movement to the northwest. Three times the chestnut tried unsuccessfully to halt them so that the colt could rest and have a fighting chance of keeping up. But some deep instinctive drive within the herd kept luring them away from their homeland, and soon it lay far behind them. The dun-colored mare did her best to keep the colt beside her, and he ran with ungainly legs to stay close. She was pleased to see that he grew stronger each day and that his legs functioned better as they moved onto higher ground.

"But in the fifth week, as they approached a cold part of their journey, food became scarce and the wisdom of this trek, doubtful. Then the herd had to scatter to find forage, and one evening as the chestnut and the mare and their colt nosed among the scrub for signs of grass, a group of dire wolves struck at them. The mare intuitively presented herself to the wolves in an effort to protect her colt, but the fierce gray beasts were not deluded by this trick, and cut behind her and made savage lunges at it. This enraged the chestnut, who sprang at the wolves with flashing hoofs, but to no avail. Mercilessly, the wolves cut down the colt. His piteous cries sounded for a moment, then died in harrowing gurgle as his own blood drowned him.

"The mare was distraught and tried to attack the wolves, but six of them detached themselves and formed a pack to destroy her. She defended herself valiantly for some moments while her mate battled with the other wolves at the body of the colt. Then one bold wolf caught her by a hamstring and brought her down. In a moment the others were upon her, tearing her to pieces.

"The whole group of wolves now turned their attention to the chestnut, but he broke loose from

them and started at a mad gallop back toward where the main herd of horses had been. The wolves followed him for a few miles, then gave up the chase and returned to their feast.

"Mammals, unlike reptiles, had some capacity for memory, and as the trek to the northwest continued, the chestnut felt sorrow at the loss of his mate and the colt, but the recollection did not last long, and he was soon preoccupied with the problems of the journey.

"It was a strange hegira on which the horses of Centennial were engaged. It would take them across thousands of miles and onto land that had been under water only a few centuries earlier. For this was the age of ice. From the north pole to Pennsylvania and Wisconsin and Wyoming vast glaciers crept, erasing whatever vegetation had developed there and carving the landscape into new designs.

"At no point on earth were the changes more dramatic than at the Bering Sea, that body of ice-cold water which separates Asia from America. The great glaciers used up so much ocean water that the level of this sea dropped three hundred feet. This eliminated the Bering Sea altogether, and in its place appeared a massive land bridge more than a thousand miles wide. It was an isthmus, really, joining two continents, and now any animal that wished, or man, too, when he came along, could walk with security from Asia to America— or the other way.

"The bridge, it must be understood, was not constructed along that slim chain of islands which now reaches from America to Asia. Not at all. The drop of ocean was so spectacular that it was the main body of Asia that was joined substantially to America; the bridge was wider than the entire compass of Alaska.

"It was toward the direction of this great bridge, barely existent when the true horse emerged, that the chestnut now headed. In time, as older horses died off, he became acknowledged leader of the herd, the one who trotted at the head on leisurely marches to new meadows, the one who marshaled the herd together when danger threatened. He grew canny in the arts of leadership, homing on the good pastures, seeking out the protected resting places.

"As the horses marched to the new bridge in the northwest, to their right in unending progression lay the snouts of the glaciers, now a mile away, later on, a hundred miles distant, but always pressing southward and commandeering meadowlands where horses had previously grazed. Perhaps it was this inexorable pressure of ice from the north, eating up all good land, that had started the horses on their emigration; certainly it was a reminder that food was getting scarce throughout their known world.

"One year, as the herd moved ever closer to the beginning of the bridge, the horses were competing for food with a large herd of camels that were also deserting the land where they had originated. The chestnut, now a mature horse, led his charges well to the north, right into the face of the glacier. It was the warm period of the year and the 139 nose of the glacier was dripping, so that the horses had much good water and there was, as he had expected, good green grass.

"But as they grazed, idling the summer away before they returned to the shoreline, where they would be once more in competition with the camels, he happened to peer into a small canyon that had formed in the ice, and with four companions he penetrated it, finding to his pleasure that it contained much sweet grass. They were grazing with no apprehension when suddenly he looked up to see before him a most gigantic mammoth. It was as tall as three horses, and its mighty tusks were like none he had seen at the pillars. These tusks did not stretch forward, but turned parallel to the face in immense sweeping circles that met before the eyes.

"The chestnut stood for a moment surveying the large beast. He was not afraid, for mammoths did not attack horses, and even if for some unfathomable reason this one did, the chestnut could easily escape. And then slowly, as if the idea were incomprehensible, the stallion began to realize that under no circumstances could this particular mammoth charge, for it was dead. Its frozen rear quarters were caught in the icy grip of the glacier; its front half, from which the glacier had melted, seemed alive. It was a beast in suspension. It was there, with all its features locked in ice, but at the same time it was not there.

"Perplexed the chestnut whinnied and his companions ambled up. They looked at the im-prisoned beast, expecting it to charge, and only belatedly did each discover for himself that for some reason he could not explain, this mammoth was immobilized. One of the younger horses probed with his muzzle, but the silent mammoth gave no response. The young horse became angry and nudged the huge beast, again with no results. The horse started to whinny; then they all realized that this great beast was dead. Like all horses, they were appalled by death and silently withdrew.

"The chestnut alone wanted to investigate this mystery, and in succeeding days he returned timorously to the small canyon, still puzzled, still captivated by a situation that could not be understood. In the end he knew nothing, so he kicked his heels at the silent mammoth, returned to the grassy area, and led his herd back toward to main road to Asia.

"It must not be imagined that the horses emigrated to Asia in any steady progression. The distance from the twin pillars to Siberia was only 3500 miles, and since a horse could cover twenty-five miles a day, the trip might conceivably have been completed in less than a year, but it did not work that way. The horses never chose their direction; they merely sought easier pasturage and sometimes a herd would languish in one favorite spot for eight or nine years. They were pulled slowly westward by mysterious forces, and no horse that started from the twin pillars ever got close to Asia.

"But drift was implacable, and the chestnut

spent his years from three to sixteen in this overpowering journey, always tending toward the northwest, for the time of the horse in America was ended.

"They spent four years on the approaches to Alaska, and now the chestnut had to extend himself to keep pace with the younger horses. Often he fell behind, but he knew no fear, confident that an extra burst of effort would enable him to regain the herd. He watched as younger horses took the lead, giving the signals for marching and halting. The grass seemed thinner this year, and more difficult to find.

"One day, late in the afternoon, he was foraging in sparse lands when he became aware that the main herd—indeed the whole herd—had moved on well beyond him. He raised his head with some difficulty, for his breathing had grown tighter, to see that a pack of dire wolves had interposed itself between him and the herd. He looked about quickly for an alternate route, but those available would lead him farther from the other horses; he knew he could outrun the wolves, but he did not wish to increase the distance between himself and the herd.

"He therefore made a daring, zigzag dash right through the wolves and toward the other horses. He kicked his heels and with surprising speed negotiated a good two-thirds of the distance through the snarling wolves. Twice he heard jaws snapping at his forelocks, but he managed to kick free.

"Then, with terrible suddenness, his breath came short and a great pain clutched at his chest. He fought against it, kept pumping his legs. He felt his body stopping almost in midflight, stopping while the wolves closed in to grab his legs. He felt a sharp pain radiating from his hind quarters where two wolves had fastened onto him, but this external wolf-pain was of lesser consequence than the interior horse-pain that clutched at him. If only his breath could be maintained, he could throw off the wolves. He had done so before. But now the greater pain assailed him and he sank slowly to earth as the pack fell upon him.

"The last thing he saw was the uncomprehending herd, following younger leaders, as it maintained its glacial course toward Asia.

"Why did this stallion that had prospered so in Colorado desert his amiable homeland for Siberia? We do not know. Why did the finest animal America developed become discontented with the land of his origin? There is no answer. We know that when the horse negotiated the land bridge, which he did with apparent ease and in considerable numbers, he found on the other end an opportunity for varied development that is one of the bright aspects of animal history. He wandered into France and became the mighty Percheron, and into Arabia, where he developed into a lovely poem of a horse, and into Africa, where he became the brilliant zebra, and into Scotland, where he bred selectively to form the massive Clydesdale. He would also journey into Spain, where his very name would become the designation for gen- 141 tleman, a caballero, a man of the horse. There he would flourish mightily and serve the armies that would conquer much of the known world, and in 1519 he would leave Spain in small adventurous ships of conquest and land in Mexico, where he would thrive and develop special characteristics fitting him for life on upland plains. In 1543 he would accompany Coronado on his quest for the golden cities of Quivira, and from later groups of horses brought by other Spaniards some would be stolen by Indians and a few would escape to become feral, once domesticated but now reverted to wildness. And from these varied sources would breed the animals that would return late in history, in the year 1768, to Colorado, the land from which they had sprung, making it for a few brief years the kingdom of the horse, the memorable epitome of all that was best in the relationship of horse and man.''

In the years that followed that profound experience in the Denver Museum with James Michener, my passion for horses would take me to places that were often as exciting and exotic as were the animals that I was studying and photographing. On more than one occasion, as I watched the rising sun red-orange the marsh water around my rubber boots to the brilliance of molten lava, or as at sunset I stretched out on the desert sand which was wind-rippled and moving to create a pageant of overwhelming beauty, my thoughts would turn to one of the most important first friendly encounters, or introductions, of two living creatures in the history of this planet—that of man and horse.

Time after time my imagination would play with that first prehistoric rendezvous before which equines had meant only food and clothing to man, not friendship, utility, and sport. Then the horse was to be killed, eaten, its hide used for garments and shelter; its bones for utensils and weapons; and its blood and body fluids for decoration, not only of the hunter's own skin, but for re-creating the dead animal in cave paintings of such beauty that many of those that survive are among the most magnificent works of art ever produced by man.

Disappointingly, while I researched scores of books for quotations that would accompany the photographs in *Equus* and *Stallion of a Dream*, never did I chance upon any sort of fictional description of a prehistoric encounter between horse and man except as prey and hunter. What were the circumstances of their first friendly encounter?

Although there must have been any number of ways in which prehistoric hunters killed equines, some methods are more obvious than others. It is known that horses were stampeded toward and off high cliffs after which the dead could be skinned and butchered while the injured were slaughtered. Individual animals were also killed in the act of mating, hamstrung by the hunters who had crept up on them. More inventive and industrious cavemen possibly dug pits into which horses were frightened, although it was simpler to drive a stallion and his harem into a box canyon where they

could be stoned or speared to death.

Following one of these hunts, among the dead animals we imagine a foal who in spite of his size—or because of it—had survived the massacre. Seeking warmth and companionship, it follows after a human busy skinning and cutting meat from a dead stallion. The hunter lifts his spear to kill the pathetic foal—to be stopped by a fellow tribesman who realizes there are already more skins and meat than can be carried.

As the tribe moves away from the bloodied remains of the dead horses, the foal, attracted by the large and moving human shapes—pulled by the magnetic herd instinct—follows after them.

Later, when the tribe stops to rest, the humans are amused and amazed at how the foal sucks their fingers. One of the women then takes a gourd full of grain brew and allows the liquid to dribble down her hand and fingers, to feed the baby animal. And so it may have been that the horse was domesticated.

At what point in time a man first sat on a horse's back, we do not know. But finally that supreme moment did arrive. A human being. A horse. The first ride! Up until that moment, most certainly even the wildest of dreams had never sped a person above the ground with such velocity and power. Perhaps this was man's first adventure with flight.

When the first domestic equine was called by any other tribal sound but "horse" is another mystery of time. But, as man's imagination developed, some light-colored animal must have reminded him of snow or clouds and was thereafter so called. Another, because of its speed, may have been known as Wind; a black-haired animal symbolized smoke or night and from that moment was summoned by that name.

So, it probably was that in prehistory the horse was domesticated and from that moment, until a mere hundred years ago, few important military battles would be won, nor would an important civilization be established in which the hoofprints of equines did not precede those of man.

And of the world's great conquerors, none can match the exploits of Alexander the Great. Never has recorded history described a soldier of such genius, and the seat from which he commanded his armies was the back of a black stallion unromantically named Oxhead or Bucephalus. Not only did Alexander adore Bucephalus, but there seems to have existed between them as much feeling as is possible between man and horse. How Alexander acquired Bucephalus is an often-told story, but no one relates it better than does Mary Renault in *Fire from Heaven:*

"'One can't know too much of Xenophon,' Alexander said, 'When it comes to horses. I want to read his books about Persia, too. Are you buying anything today?'

"'Not this year. My brother's buying one.'

"'Xenophon says a good hoof ought to make a ringing noise like a cymbal. That one there looks splay to me. My father wants a new battle-charger. 143

He had one killed under him, fighting the Illyrians last year.' He looked at the dais beside them, run up as usual for the spring horse-fair; the King had not yet arrived.

"It was a sharp brilliant day; the lake and the lagoon were ruffled and darkly gleaming; the white clouds that skimmed across to the distant mountains had edges honed blue, like swords. The bruised turf of the meadow was green from the winter rains. All morning the soldiers had been buying; officers for themselves, tribal chiefs for the vassals who made up their squadrons (in Macedon, the feudal and regimental always overlapped), tough stocky thick-maned beasts, lively and sleek from the winter grazing. By noon, this common business was done; now the bloodstock was coming out, racers and parade show-horses and chargers, curried and dressed up to the eyes.

"The horse fair at Pella was a rite not less honored than the sacred feasts. Dealers came from the horse-lands of Thessaly, from Thrace, from Epiros, even across Hellespont; these would always claim their stock was crossed with the fabled Nisaian strain of the Persian kings.

"Important buyers were only now arriving. Alexander had been there most of the day. Following him about, not yet at least with him or with one another, were half a dozen boys whom Philip had lately collected from fathers he wished to honor. . . .

"The morning, however, of the horse fair, he had been spending with the boys attached to him by the King. He had been pleased to have their company; if he treated them all as his juniors, it was not to assert himself or put them down, but because he never felt it otherwise. He had talked horses untiringly, and they had done their best to keep up. His sword belt, his fame, and the fact that with all this he was the smallest of them, bewildered them and made them awkward. They were relieved that now, for the showing of the bloodstock, his friends were gathering. Ptolemy and Harpalos and Philotas and the rest. Left on one side, they clumped together and, with their pack-leader gone, started edging for precedence like a chance-met group of dogs.

"'My father couldn't come in today. It's not worth it; he imports his horses straight from Thessaly. All the breeders know him.'

"'I shall need a bigger horse soon; but my father's leaving it till next year, when I've grown taller.'

"'Alexander's a hand shorter than you, and *he* rides men's horses.'

"'Oh, well, I expect they trained them specially.'

"The tallest of the boys said, 'He took his boar. I suppose you think they trained a boar for him.' . . .

"The horse fair was always easy-going, an outing where men were men. Philip in riding-clothes lifted his switch to the lords and squires and officers and horse-dealers; mounted the stand, shouted to this friend or that to join him. His eye fell on his son; he made a movement, then saw the little court around him and turned away. Alexander picked up his talk with Harpalos, a dark lively good-looking youth with much offhand charm, whom fate had cursed with a clubfoot. Alexander had always admired the way he bore it.

"A racehorse came pounding by, ridden by a little Nubian boy in a striped tunic. Word had gone round that this year the King was only in the market for a battle-charger; but he had paid the sum, already a legend, of thirteen talents for the racer that had won for him at Olympia; and the dealer had thought it worth a try. Philip smiled and shook his head; the Nubian boy, who had hoped to be bought with the horse, to wear gold earrings and eat meat of feast-days, cantered back, his face a landscape of grief.

"The chargers were led up, in precedence fiercely fought over by the dealers all the forenoon, and settled in the end by substantial bribes. The King came down to peer into mouths and at upturned hooves, to feel shanks and listen to chests. The horses were led away, or kept by in case nothing better turned up. There was a lag. Philip looked impatiently about. The big Thessalian dealer, Philonikos, who had been fuming for some time, said to his runner, 'Tell them I'll have their guts for picket ropes, if they don't bring the beast *now*.'

"'Kittos says, sir, they can *bring* him, but . . .'

"'I had to break the brute myself, must I show him too? Tell Kittos from me, if I miss this sale,

they won't have hide enough left between them for a pair of sandal soles.' With a sincere, respectful smile, he approached the King. 'Sir, he's on his way. You'll see he's all I wrote you from Larissa, and more. Forgive the delay; they've just now told me, some fool let him slip his tether. In prime fettle as he is, he was hard to catch. Ah! Here he comes now.'

"They led up, at a careful walk, a black with a white blaze. The other horses had been ridden, to show their paces. Though he was certainly in a sweat, he did not breathe like a horse that had been running. When they pulled him up before the King and his horse-trainer, his nostrils flared and his black eye rolled sidelong; he tried to rear his head, but the groom dragged it down. His bridle was costly, red leather trimmed with silver; but he had no saddlecloth. The dealer's lips moved viciously in his beard.

"A hushed voice beside the dais said, 'Look, Ptolemy. Look at *that*.'

"'There, sir!' said Philonikos, forcing rapture into his voice. "There's Thunder. If there ever stepped a mount fit for a King . . .'

"He was indeed, at all points, the ideal horse of Xenophon. Starting, as he advises, with the feet, one saw that the horns of the hooves were deep before and behind; when he stamped, as he was doing now (just missing the groom's foot) they made a ringing sound like a cymbal. His leg-bones were strong but flexible; his chest was broad, his neck arched, as the writer puts it, like a 145 gamecock's; the mane was long, strong, silky and badly combed. His back was firm and wide, the spine well padded, his loins were short and broad. His black coat shone; on one flank was branded the horned triangle, the Oxhead, which was the mark of his famous breed. Strikingly, his forehead had a white blaze which almost copied its shape.

"'That,' said Alexander with awe, 'is a perfect horse. Perfect everywhere.'

"'He's vicious,' Ptolemy said.

"Over at the horse-lines, the chief groom Kittos said to a fellow slave who had watched their struggles. 'Days like this, I wish they'd cut my throat along with my father's, when they took our town. My back's not healed from last time and he'll be at me again before sundown.'

"'That horse is a murderer. What does he want, does he want to kill the King?'

"'There was nothing wrong with that horse, I tell you nothing, nothing beyond high spirits, till he lost his temper when it took against him. He's like a wild beast in his drink; mostly it's us men he takes it out of, we come cheaper than horses. Now it's anyone's fault but his; he'd kill me if I told him its temper's spoiled for good. He only bought it from Kroisos a month ago, just for this deal. Two talents he paid.' His bearer whistled. 'He reckoned to get three, and he well might if he'd not set out to break its heart. It's held out well, I'll say that for it. He broke mine long ago.'

"Philip, seeing the horse was restive, walked round it a few paces away. 'Yes, I like his looks. Well, let's see him move.'

"Philonikos took a few steps toward the horse. It gave a squeal like a battle-trumpet, forced up its head against the hanging weight of the groom, and pawed the air. The dealer swore and kept his distance; the groom got the horse in hand. As if dye were running from the red bridle, a few drops of blood fell from its mouth.

"Alexander said, 'Look at that bit they've put on him. Look at those barbs.'

"'It seems even that can't hold him,' said big Philotas easily. 'Beauty's not everything.'

"'And still he got his head up.' Alexander had moved forward. The men strolled after, looking out after him; he barely reached Philotas' shoulder.

"'You can see his spirit, sir,' Philonikos told the King eagerly. 'A horse like this, one could train to rear up and strike the enemy.'

"'The quickest way to have your mount killed under you,' said Philip brusquely, 'making it show its belly.' He beckoned the leathery bow-legged man attending him. 'Will you try him, Jason?'

"The royal trainer walked round to the front of the horse, making cheerful soothing sounds. It backed, stamped and rolled its eyes. He clicked his tongue, saying firmly, 'Thunder, boy, hey, Thunder.' At the sound of its name it seemed to quiver all over with suspicion and rage. 'Keep his head till I'm up,' he told the groom, 'that looks like one man's work.' He approached the horse's side, ready to reach for the roots of the mane; the only means, unless a man had a spear to vault on, of getting up. The saddlecloth, had it been on, would have offered comfort and show, but no kind of foothold. A hoist was for the elderly, and Persians, who were notoriously soft.

"At the last moment, his shadow passed before the horse's eyes. It gave a violent start, swerved, and lashed out, missing Jason by inches. He stepped back and squinted at it sideways, screwing up one eye and the side of his mouth. The King met his look and raised his eyebrows.

"Alexander, who had been holding his breath, looked round at Ptolemy and said in a voice of anguish, 'He won't buy him.'

"'Who would?' said Ptolemy surprised. 'Can't think why he was shown. Xenophon wouldn't have bought him. You were quoting him only just now, how the nervous horse won't let you harm the enemy, but he'll do plenty of harm to you.'

"'Nervous? He? He's the bravest horse I ever saw. He's a fighter. Look where he's been beaten, under the belly too, you can see the weals. If Father doesn't buy him, that man will flay him alive. I can see it in his face.'

"Jason tried again. Before he got anywhere near the horse it started kicking. He looked at the King, who shrugged his shoulders.

"'It was his shadow,' said Alexander urgently to Ptolemy. 'He's shy of his own, even. Jason should have seen.'

"'He's seen enough; he's got the King's life to think of. Would you ride a horse like that to war?'

"'Yes, I would. To war most of all.'

"Philotas raised his brows, but failed to catch Ptolemy's eye.

"'Well, Philonikos,' said Philip, 'if that's the pick of your stable, let's waste no more time. I've work to do.'

"'Sir, give us a moment. He's frisky for want of exercise; too full of corn. With his strength, he—'

"'I can buy something better for three talents than a broken neck.'

"'My lord, for you only, I'll make a special price.'

"'I'm busy,' Philip said.

"Philonikos set his thick mouth in a wide straight line. The groom, hanging for dear life on the spiked bit, began to turn the horse for the horse-lines. Alexander called out in his high carrying voice, 'What a waste! The best horse in the show!'

"Anger and urgency gave it a note of arrogance that made heads turn. Philip looked round startled. Never, at the worst of things, had the boy been rude to him in public. It had best be ignored till later. The groom and the horse were moving off.

"'The best horse ever shown here, and all he needs is handling.' Alexander had come out into the field. All his friends, even Ptolemy, left a discreet space round him; he was going too far. The whole crowd was staring. 'A horse in ten thousand, just thrown away.'

"Philip, looking again, decided the boy had not meant to be so insolent. He was a colt too full of corn, ever since his two precocious exploits. They had gone to his head. No lesson so good, thought Philip, as the one a man teaches to himself. 'Jason here,' he said, 'has been training horses for twenty years. And you, Philonikos; how long?' 147

"The dealer's eyes shifted from father to son; he was on a tightrope. 'Ah, well, sir, I was reared to it from a boy.'

"'You hear that, Alexander? But you think you can do better?'

"Alexander glanced, not at his father but at Philonikos. With an unpleasant sense of shock, the dealer looked away.

"'Yes. With this horse, I could.'

"'Very well,' said Philip. 'If you can, he's yours.'

"The boy looked at the horse, with parted lips and devouring eyes. The groom had paused with it. It snorted over its shoulder.

"'And if you can't?' said the King briskly. 'What are you staking?'

"Alexander took a deep breath, his eyes not leaving the horse. 'If I can't ride him, I'll pay for him myself.'

"Philip raised his dark heavy brows. 'At three talents?' The boy had only just been put up to a youth's allowance; it would take most of this year's, and the next as well.

"'Yes,' Alexander said.

"'I hope you mean it. I do.'

"'So do I.' Roused from his single concern with the horse, he saw that everyone was staring: the officers, the chiefs, the grooms and dealers, Ptolemy and Harpalos and Philotas; the boys he had spent the morning with. The tall one, Hephaistion, who moved so well that he always caught the eye, had stepped out before the other. For a moment their looks met.

"Alexander smiled at Philip. 'It's a bet then, Father. He's mine; and the loser pays.' There was a buzz of laughter and applause in the royal circle, born of relief that it had turned good-humored. Only Philip, who had caught it full in the eyes, had known it for a battle-smile, save for one watcher of no importance who had known it too.

"Philonikos, scarcely able to credit this happy turn of fate, hastened to overtake the boy, who was making straight for the horse. Since he could not win, it was important he should not break his neck. It would be too much to hope that the King would settle up for him.

"'My lord, you'll find that—'

"Alexander looked round and said, 'Go away.'

"'But, my lord, when you come to—'

"'Go away. Over there, down wind, where he can't see you or smell you. You've done enough.'

"Philonikos looked into the paled and widened eyes. He went, in silence, exactly where he was told.

"Alexander remembered, then, that he had not asked when the horse was first called Thunder, or if it had had another name. It had said plainly enough that Thunder was the name for tyranny and pain. It must have a new name, then. He walked round, keeping his shadow behind, looking at the horned blaze under the blowing forelock.

"'Oxhead,' he said, falling into Macedonian, the speech of truth and love. 'Boukephalos, Boukephalos.'

"The horse's ears went up. At the sound of this voice, the hated presence had lost power and

been driven away. What now? It had lost all trust in men. It snorted, and pawed the ground in warning.

"Ptolemy said, 'The King may be sorry he set him on to this.'

"'He was born lucky,' said Philotas. 'Do you want to bet?'

"Alexander said to the groom, 'I'll take him. You needn't wait.'

"'Oh, no, sir! When you're mounted, my lord. My lord, they'll hold me accountable.'

"'No, he's mine now. Just give me his head without jerking that bit . . . I said, give it to me. *Now*.'

"He took the reins, easing them at first only a little. The horse snorted, then turned and snuffed at him. The off forefoot raked restlessly. He took the reins in one hand, to run the other along the moist neck; then shifted his grip to the headstall, so that the barbed bit no longer pressed at all. The horse only pulled forward a little. He said to the groom, 'Go that way. Don't cross the light.'

"He pushed round the horse's head to face the bright spring sun. Their shadows fell out of sight behind them. The smell of its sweat and breath and leather bathed him in its steam. 'Boukephalos,' he said softly.

"It strained forward, trying to drag him with it; he took in the rein a little. A horsefly was on its muzzle; he ran his hand down, till his fingers felt the soft lip. Almost pleadingly now, the horse urged them both onward, as if saying, 'Come quickly away from here.'

"'Yes, yes,' he said stroking its neck. 'All in good time, when I say, we'll go. You and I don't run away.'

"He had better take off his cloak; while he spared a hand for the pin, he talked on to keep the horse in mind of him. 'Remember who we are. Alexander and Boukephalos.'

"The cloak fell behind him; he slid his arm over the horse's back. It must be near fifteen hands, a tall horse for Greece; he was used to fourteen. This one was as tall as Philotas' horse about which he talked so much. The black eye rolled round at him. 'Easy, easy, now. I'll tell you when.'

"With the reins looped in his left hand he grasped the arch of the mane; with his right, its base between the shoulders. He could feel the horse gather itself together. He ran a few steps with it to gain momentum, then leaped, threw his right leg over; he was up.

"The horse felt the light weight on its back, compact of certainty; the mercy of invincible hands, the forbearance of immovable will; a nature it knew and shared, transfigured to divinity. Men had not mastered it; but it would go with the god.

"The crowd was silent at first. They were men who knew horses, and had more sense than to startle this one. In a breathing hush they waited for it to get its head, taking for granted the boy would be run away with, eager to applaud if he could only stick on and ride it to a standstill. But he had it in hand; it was waiting his sign to go. There was a hum of wonder; then, when they saw him lean forward and kick his heel with a shout, when boy and horse went racing down towards the water-meadows, the roar began. They vanished into the distance; only the rising clouds of wildfowl showed where they had gone.

"They came back at last with the sun behind them, their shadow thrown clear before. Like the feet of a carved pharaoh treading his beaten enemies, the drumming hooves trampled the shadow triumphantly into the ground.

"At the horse-field they slowed to a walk. The horse blew and shook its bridle. Alexander sat easy, in the pose which Xenophon commends: the legs straight down, gripping with the thigh, relaxed below the knee. He rode towards the stand; but a man stood waiting down in front of it. It was his father.

"He swung off cavalry style, across the neck with his back to the horse; considered the best way in war, if the horse allowed it. The horse was remembering things learned before the tyranny. Philip put out both arms; Alexander came down into them. 'Look out we don't jerk his mouth, Father,' he said. 'It's sore.'

"Philip pounded him on the back. He was weeping. Even his blind eye wept real tears. 'My son!' he said choking. There was wet in his harsh beard. 'Well done, my son, my son.'

"Alexander returned his kiss. It seemed to him that this was a moment nothing could undo. 'Thank you, Father. Thank you for my horse. I shall call him Oxhead.'

"The horse gave a sudden start. Philonikos was coming up, beaming and full of compliments. Alexander looked round, and motioned with his head. Philonikos withdrew. The buyer was never wrong.

"A surging crowd had gathered. 'Will you tell them to keep off, Father? He won't stand people yet. I'll have to rub him down myself, or he'll catch a chill.'

"He saw to the horse, keeping the best of the grooms beside him for it to know him another time. The crowd was still in the horse-field. All was quiet in the stable yard when he came out, flushed from the ride and the work, tousled, smelling of horse."

Later in her book, Mary Renault testifies to the special relationship between the boy and the stallion when she describes Alexander's introduction to Aristotle:

"Presentations went forward, the Prince performing them with address. A groom led up a mount for the philosopher, offering a leg up, Persian style. This seen to, the boy turned round; a taller boy moved forward, his hand on the head-stall of a magnificent black charger with a white blaze. All through the formalities, Aristotle had been aware of the creature fretting; he was surprised therefore to see the youth release it. It trotted straight to the Prince, and muzzled the hair behind his ear. He stroked it, murmuring something. With neatness and dignity, the horse sank its crupper on its haunches, waited while he mounted, and at his finger-touch straightened up.

There was a moment in which the boys and the beast seemed like initiates, who have exchanged in secret a word of power.

"The philosopher swept aside this fantasy. Nature had no mysteries, only facts not yet correctly observed and analyzed. Proceed from this sound first principle, and one would never miss one's way."

In her sequel novel, *The Persian Boy*, Mary Renault shows us a Bucephalus, worn by age yet loved no less by Alexander:

"Next morning there was a stir of expectation in the camp. I joined the crowd near the royal tent, though I had wakened with a headache. Seeing that the old Macedonian near me had a kindly face, I asked who was arriving. He said smiling, 'Boukephalos. The Mardians are bringing him back.'

"'Boukephalos?' Surely this meant Oxhead; an odd name. 'Who is he, please?'

"'You have never heard of Oxhead? Why, Alexander's horse.'

"Remembering how satrap after satrap had brought him steeds matchless in their kinds, I asked why the Mardians were bringing this one. He answered, 'Because they stole him.'

"'In that horse-thief country,' I said, 'the King was lucky to get him back so soon.'

"'It had to be soon,' said the old man calmly. 'Alexander sent word that if he were not returned, he would fire the forests and put them all to the sword.'

"'For a *horse*?' I cried, remembering his kindness to Artabazos, his mercy to the Greeks. 'But he would never really have done it?'

"The old man considered. 'For Oxhead? Oh, yes, I think so. Not all at once. He would have begun, and gone on till they brought him back.'

"The King had come out, and was standing before his tent, as he'd done to welcome Artabazos. Hephaistion and Ptolemy stood by him. Ptolemy was a bony-faced warrior with a broken nose, some ten years older than Alexander. Most Persian kings would have had such a person put out of the way when they assumed the throne; but these two seemed the best of friends. At the sound of approaching horns, all three were smiling.

"A Mardian chief came first, in an ancient robe which looked as if it had been stolen in Artaxerxes' day. Behind was the string of horses. I saw at once there was not a Nisaian among them; but size is not everything.

"I craned over all the shoulders, to glimpse this peerless pearl, this arrow of fire, that was worth a province and its people. He must be such, for the King even to have missed him, among so many. Darius had always been superbly mounted, and would soon have noticed a falling off; but it was the Master of the Stables who knew which was which.

"The cavalcade approached. The Mardians, in token of repentance, had adorned all the horses with their barbaric finery, plumes on their heads, on their foreheads nets of scarlet wool, glittering

with beads and sequins. For some reason, they had made gaudiest of all an old black horse that was plodding along in front, looking dead-beat. The King took a few steps forward.

"The old beast threw up its head and whinnied loudly; you could see, then, it had been a good horse once. Suddenly Ptolemy, running like a boy, took its bridle from the Mardian, and loosed it. It broke into a stiff-legged canter, all its foolish fripperies jingling; made straight for the King, and nuzzled against his shoulder.

"The King stroked its nose a time or two. He had been standing, it seemed all this time grasping an apple, and with this he fed it. Then he turned round with his face pressed to its neck. I saw that he was crying.

"There seemed nothing, now, with which he could still astonish me. I looked round at the soldiers, to see how they would take it. Beside me, two weathered Macedonians were blinking and wiping their noses.

"The horse had been pushing at the King's ear, as if to confide in him. Now it sank creaking on its haunches. This done, it sat like one who has achieved something, and expects reward.

"The King, his cheeks still wet, said, 'He's too stiff for this. He will keep it up. I'll never get him out of it.' He bestrode the saddlecloth. The horse heaved itself up quite briskly. They trotted off towards the stables. The assembled army gave a cheer; the King turned and waved.

"The old man by me turned to me with a smile. I said, 'I don't understand, sir. Why, that

horse looks to be well past twenty.'

"'Oh, yes. It is twenty-five; a year younger than Alexander. It was meant to be sold to his father, when he was thirteen. It had been mistreated on the way, and would let no one near it. King Philip would have none of it. It was Alexander who cried out that a great horse was being thrown away. His father thought him too forward, and gave him leave to try, thinking it would humble him. But it trusted him, as soon as it felt his hand. Yes, that was the first time he did what his father could not . . . He had his first command at sixteen, and before that he was at war; all that time, he has ridden Oxhead. Even at Gaugamela, he saved him up for the charge, though he changed horses soon after. Well, Oxhead has fought his last battle. But as you see, he is still beloved.'

"'That is rare,' I said, 'in kings.'

"'In anyone. . . .'

"Since the capture of his old horse Oxhead, the King was displeased with his squires. His horses were their charge; they had been leading them through the forests, when the Mardians fell on them. They had reported themselves vastly outnumbered; but Alexander, who spoke Thracian, had had a word with the grooms. They, being unarmed, had had no face to save. He was still nursing Oxhead like a favorite child, taking him out each day in case he should be pining. He had pictured him, no doubt, ending his days as a half-starved beast of burden, beaten, and full of harness sores."

The Persian boy then offers us yet another in-

sight into Alexander's esteem for Bucephalus, or Oxhead:

"The only upshot of this, that I could see, was his looking at Oxathres' horse-trappings, and liking them so much that he had them copied for old Oxhead. No Greek horse looks wonderful to a Persian; but now he was fed, tended and fresh, you could believe he had carried Alexander in battle for ten years and never once shown fear. Most horses would have been bothered by the new finery, the headstall with the cockade, the silver cheekpieces and the hanging plaques on the collar; but Oxhead thought very well of himself, and paced along making the most of them. There was a good deal in him of Alexander."

Though Alexander died a young man and Oxhead died an old horse, it was the youth-king who powerfully survived his stallion companion:

"On one of these days, some person of consequence, whose name and race I forget, came to Alexander's tent for audience. He had been gone some time, so I said I would go and find him. I rode about the camp—no Persian will walk when he can ride—till I heard he had gone to the horse-lines. I went over to the endless rows of shelters, made from bamboo and grass and palm-leaves, which housed the cavalry mounts; a town in itself. At last a blue-tattooed Thracian slave, who was holding the King's charger, pointed me out a shelter standing alone, and handsomer than the rest. I dismounted and went inside.

"After the Indian sun it seemed almost dark. Splinters of dazzle came through the chinks of the wall, making bars of light and shade. They fell on an old black horse, that lay in the straw with laboring sides; and on Alexander, sitting in the muck of the stable floor, with its head laid in his lap.

"My shadow had darkened the doorway; he looked up.

"I had no words. I just thought, I would do anything . . . As if I had had the words all along, I said, 'Shall I fetch Hephaistion?'

"He answered, 'Thank you, Bagoas.' I could just hear him. He'd not called the groom, because he could not command his voice. So I was not there for nothing.

"I found Hephaistion by the river, among his engineers. They had brought his bridge-boats overland, in halves for cartage; he was seeing them put together. He stared at me in surprise; no doubt I looked out of place there. Besides, it was the first time I'd ever sought him out.

"'Hephaistion,' I said, 'Oxhead is dying. Alexander wants you there.'

"He looked at me in silence. Maybe he would have expected me to send someone else. Then he said, 'Thank you, Bagoas,' in a voice he'd not used to me before, and called for his horse. I let him get well ahead, before I took the road.

"Oxhead's funeral was held that evening; it has to be quick, in India. Alexander had him burned on a pyre, so as to have his ashes for a proper tomb. He only told his friends; but it was wonderful how many old soldiers came quietly up, who had fought at Issos, and Granikos, and Gaugamela. There were bowls of incense to throw 153 upon the pyre; we must have given old Oxhead a full talent's worth. Some of Omphis' Indians, who stood further off, uttered loud cries to their gods, thinking Alexander had sacrificed the horse for victory.

"When the fire had sunk, he went about his work again. But at night, I saw he looked older. When he first had Peritas he had been a man; Oxhead, he had had since boyhood. That little horse (all Greek horses look little to a Persian) had known things of him I'd never known. That day some of them died, and I shall never know them."

I can think of no other city in the world having been named for a horse except the one Alexander honored and called after his black stallion. The Persian boy refers to this when for the last time, he mentions Bucephalus:

"King Poros' flesh wound soon healed, and Alexander feasted him. He was magnificent, still in his thirties though with sons of fighting age, for the Indians marry young. I danced for him, and he gave me some ruby earrings. To Alexander's pleasure, the faithful elephant, scar-seamed from earlier wars, recovered, too.

"There were victory games, and thank-offerings to the gods. Just when the victims had been consumed, the rain came down again and doused the fires. I had never grown used to watching the divine flame polluted with burning flesh; not is any Persian easy when he sees it quenched from the sky. But I said nothing.

"The King founded two cities, one each side

the river. He named the right-bank one for Oxhead; his tomb was to be in the public square, with his statue cast in bronze."

For centuries before and after Alexander's death, horses had been and would be bridled and saddled—domestic animals which appeared to have forever lived in harmony with man. However, advanced civilizations existed that—until a mere five hundred years ago—had never known the horse by sight or even by word. As James Michener has stated, ironically, it was the American continent, home of prehistoric equus, that would be one of the last lands to know his modern counterpart.

The part that the horse played in the Spanish conquest of Latin America was so crucial that even today, at great distance, it is difficult to justly estimate its total impact. The people of South, Central, and North America had never seen horses and, to innocent Indian eyes, the combination of Spaniard on four-legged animal produced an image so awesome that it could only have been a heaven-dispatched single being.

If I had previously let my imagination play with prehistoric man's initial friendly rendezvous with an equine, even more exciting was to envision the first confrontations between horses and American Indians. Whereas prehistoric man was well familiar with the wild and savage small, stiff-maned, dun-colored, large-eared horses of the steppes, who were as wily and difficult to approach as were the deer that roamed with them,

154

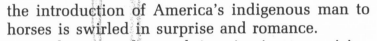

the introduction of America's indigenous man to horses is swirled in surprise and romance.

It does not take much imagination to envision a sleeping Comanche brave awakened on the night of a full moon by the sound of animal hooves—a stamping unlike that produced by any creature familiar to him. The Indian rises from his resting place and sees standing before him in the moonlight a pure white animal with shoulder-length mane and a plumed tail of such length that it touches the ground. An animal of such extraordinary and poetic beauty that it put to shame the bison, moose, elk, deer, and antelope that were then the only large ungulates to roam the American wilderness. Man and horse stand facing each other. The horse, possibly one that had broken tether and escaped from some Spanish expedition, tosses its head and moves forward toward a familiar human form. The Indian stands transfixed as the stallion steps closer. In such circumstances, one red man may have run, terrified by the approaching white apparition. Another may have grabbed his spear and thrust it into the stallion's chest or side. Yet, there is a further possibility, that the man stood his ground in awe of the glorious white beast; that from his vast knowledge of animal lore, he sensed the creature was not threatening in its approach.

The magic moment arrives. A few feet from the man, the horse stops and stretches out its neck. The velvety muzzle touches that man's bare chest. The Indian slowly raises his hands and lets them play through the strands of silken mane. And so begins a chapter that has few equals in the history of man-horse partnerships.

Only images from ancient Greece in which man was often clothed in little more than a laurel wreath and his horse barely marred by a slight bridle and reins rival aesthetically the simple beauty provided by pictures of the American Indians and their mounts. Here we have natural man, not fancied up and clothed, and almost natural horse, the animal controlled by the practically invisible war bridle—a rawhide cord looped around the horse's lower jaw, leaving the rest of the animal's head clean and free. This vision of near-naked horses and near-naked men, held together only by muscle on muscle, invokes as romantic an image as equestrian experience provides us.

The monumental influence that the horse had on the Indian way of life is described in James Michener's *Centennial:*

"The arrival of the horse among Our People changed many things. To take one example, it was now more pleasant to be a woman, for when the tribe moved she no longer had to haul the travois that were too heavy for the dogs. For another, the whole system of wealth was altered, and a man did not have to wait years to accumulate enough bison robes to procure the things he wanted; a horse was not only more acceptable as exchange but also more easily delivered when a transaction was agreed upon.

"Hunting the bison changed, too. Three men

could scout out the herd, covering immense distances, and when they found it, the whole tribe did not have to trudge in pursuit; sixteen swift-riding hunters could trail it and with arrows shoot off the animals needed, then truss up the good parts and haul them back by travois.

"The change was greatest for the dogs. They no longer had to haul huge loads on small travois. One horse could haul ten times as much on a big one, and dogs could be kept as pets until the time came for eating them.

"Our People, in bringing the horse to Rattlesnake Buttes, unwittingly returned it to the point of its genesis, and there it flourished. A gentler tribe than their neighbors, Our People had an innate appreciation of the horse, attending more carefully to its feeding and care. The saddles Our People devised were an improvement over the heavy affairs used by the Pawnee or the crude wooden efforts of the Ute. The bridles were simpler, too, with a decoration more restrained and utilitarian. Our People adopted the horse as a member of their family, and it proved a most useful friend, for it permitted them to conquer the plains, which they had already occupied but not really explored.

"On no Indian did the horse exert a more profound influence than on Lame Beaver. In 1769, when he was twenty-two, one of his fathers approached him again about marrying Blue Leaf but found him far more concerned about a horse than a wife. After the raid on the Comanche camp, the captured horses were allotted according to a sensible plan: the best-trained mounts went to the older chiefs, who needed them for ceremonial purposes; the acceptable ones went to the middle chiefs, who did the scouting for bison; and the unbroken horses went to the young warriors, who had the time to train them.

"Despite the fact that Lame Beaver had masterminded the raid, he was given a nervous, unbroken pinto mare, and when he first tried to ride her she tossed him viciously into the middle of a prairie-dog town. The little animals peeked out of their holes in chattering wonder as he limped after the pinto, failing to catch her on his first tries.

"Again and again he sweated with the stubborn pony, not much bigger than he was, and repeatedly she pitched him over her head. Others volunteered to show him how to master her, and they went flying, too. Finally an old man said 'I heard once that the Comanche do it by taking their horses into the river.'

"This was such a novel idea that Lame Beaver could not yet grasp its significance, but, after his pinto had resisted other efforts, he and his friends tied her and dragged her by main strength down to the Platte. She shied away from the water, but they plunged in, keeping hold of the thongs, got a good footing, and pulled and jerked until it looked as if her neck might come off before her stubborn feet touched water. Finally, with a mighty jerk, they got her off the bank and into the stream.

"She was very frightened, but they kept tugging at her until her beautiful white-and-black-and-brown body was mostly submerged. Then Lame Beaver swam close to her, so that his face was almost touching hers. He began to talk with her, slowly and with a reassuring tone: 'For years and years you and I will be friends. We will ride after the bison together. You will know the feel of my knees on your flanks and turn as I bid you. We shall be friends for all the years and I will see that you get grass.'

"When he had spoken with her thus, and quieted somewhat the fear in her eyes, he took off the thongs and left her in the middle of the river. Without looking at her further, he swam to the bank and climbed out. She watched him go, made a half-hearted start for the opposite bank, then followed him, but when she was again safe on land she refused to let him approach.

"Daily for two weeks Lame Beaver dragged his pinto into the river, and on the fifteenth day, there in the water, she allowed him to mount her, and when she felt the security of his strong legs about her, she responded and finally ran boldly onto the land and off toward the Rattlesnake Buttes.

"From that moment she was his companion, and she liked nothing more than to chase after bison. Since he required both hands to manipulate his bow, she learned to respond to his knee movements, and they formed a team. She was so sure-footed that he did not try to guide her, satisfied that she would find the best course, whatever the terrain. And sometimes, when he saw her running free with a group of other horses, he would catch sight of her straight back and its white patches and he would experience an emotion that could only be called love.

"He was therefore disturbed when his father came to him and said, 'The brother of Blue Leaf is willing that you should marry his sister, but he demands that you fulfill your promise and give him your horse.'

"Lame Beaver snapped, 'He has his horse . . .'

"'True, but he argues that that horse was given him by the council, not by you. For Blue Leaf, he demands your horse.'

"This outrageous request Lame Beaver refused. He still wanted Blue Leaf; certainly he had seen no other girl so attractive, but not at the price of his horse. Obstinately he declined even to discuss the matter.

"But now the council intervened: 'Lame Beaver promised to give a horse for Blue Leaf. Many heard how he made that vow. He cannot now change his mind and refuse to deliver the horse. It belongs to the brother of Blue Leaf.'

"When Lame Beaver heard this decision he was enraged, and might have done something unwise had not Red Nose come to him to speak in low, judicious tones: 'There seems no escape, old friend.'

"'I won't surrender that pinto.'

"'She is no longer yours, dear friend. Tonight they will take her away.'

"Such a verdict seemed so unjust that Lame

157

Beaver went before the council and cried, 'I will not give up my horse. Her brother doesn't even care for the one you gave him.'

"'It is proper,' said the elderly chief, 'that men should marry in an orderly way, and we have always given presents to the brothers of our brides. A horse is a suitable gift on such an occasion. Yours must be surrendered to the brother of Blue Leaf.'

"On hearing this final judgment, Lame Beaver sped from the council tipi, leaped upon the pinto and dashed from the village, heading southward toward the river. He was followed by Cottonwood Knee, riding a brown pony, and as Lame Beaver was about to spur his pinto into the river, his pursuer caught up with him.

"'Come back!' Cottonwood Knee called in the voice of friendship. 'You and I can catch many more horses.'

"'Never like this one,' Lame Beaver said bitterly, but in the end he dismounted and allowed Cottonwood Knee to lead the pinto back to its new owner. As Lame Beaver stood by the river, watching his horse disappear, a feeling of inconsolable grief came over him, and for five days he wandered alone. In the end he returned to camp, and Cottonwood Knee and Red Nose took him before the council, and they said, 'We have ordered Blue Leaf's brother to give her to you. She is now your wife.'"

Horses, however, had lasting importance to Indians, and the Pinto is never out of Lame Beaver's mind. The night before a battle with the Pawnee, the black-and-white horse returns to trample the then old Indian's thoughts:

"During the night he prayed, but not attentively, for his mind went back to just one thing, insistently: he kept seeing that first wild pinto he had captured from the Comanche and tamed in the river, only to lose it to Blue Leaf's brother. How marvelous that pinto was, how like the wind. Its handsome black and white spots were etched on his mind and he could still recall the placement of each.

"'Heigh! Go!' he cried, and the ghost horse leaped across the prairie like a ray of sunlight, illuminating everything it approached.

"'Heigh! Heigh!' he called, and the pinto ran on and on into the mountains. Tears came into the old man's eyes and he turned to his gun, but always in the distance there stood the pinto, her colors bright and her mane standing clear.

"'Come!' the old man called softly, but the pinto headed for other pastures."

For the last twelve years, as horses and the study and photographing of them have led me around the world, I have met people, some renowned, others basic country folk, who depend on equine companionship, pay tribute to and esteem their animals with no less intensity and devotion than did Alexander the Great; and there are other persons, including myself, who like Lame Beaver would be haunted by the vision of a dead horse, one that had been more than a mere animal but a part of us in the joy of having been practically one with it and the never-healing sorrow of having been separated from it.

Because of the ways of my life, hardly a day passes that I don't see an example of some man's, woman's, or child's passion for a horse, and in this I find a never-ending source of happiness and inspiration. As I have already said, though some of these persons are famous, while others are not, these men and women exemplify all that is noble in man and his relationship with other creatures. In these pages I pay tribute to some of them.

Each of these horse lovers is also an extraordinary human being. Each of them more than merits the superlatives with which they have been garlanded in this book. Though their love for horses in general is documented by their interest in the primitive behavior of the last of the world's free-living equines, each has his or her own passion for a particular breed of domestic horse. During my years of equine observation, I have come to the conclusion that no one breed is more beautiful than another—each has its own charisma. To compare a Quarter horse to an Arabian, or an Andalusian to a Clydesdale, is like trying to compare a Modigliani to a Rubens. Each painting, as does each horse, has its own style, appeal, and beauty. What each of the persons distinguished in the following pages does have in common is a passion for the animals around which their lives virtually evolve. My pleasure is to know them personally, a pleasure that can hopefully be shared here.

HECTOR AND KAREN ALCALDE

THE SPANISH SUMMER heat beat down with Saharan intensity as one Sunday I drove the long, dusty lane to the Andalusian horse farm Lerena. Though the deserts of North Africa were not terribly far away, still the sunflowers that swept off yellow on all sides and to the horizon were a reminder that this was a Mediterranean land whose fields months before had bloodied red the Andalusian landscape with poppies.

Minutes later, I was parking my car in front of the hacienda and then passing through the cool interior and inner courtyard, beyond which four handsome people sat at a table under a sunshade near the swimming pool. My hosts, Paco Lazo and his wife, Marí Tere, were there; the other couple were strangers to me. The woman, with her delicate blond beauty, I would have taken for a high-fashion model who might have been doing a shoot for *Vogue* in Marbella. The man with her had the dark good looks of a Spanish aristocrat. But of one thing I was sure—that to be at Lerena, they must love Andalusian horses as did their hosts, who are among the most distinguished breeders of these animals in Spain.

When introductions had been made, I learned that Hector Alcalde was not a Spanish aristocrat, but a Washington consultant and lobbyist; and that his blond wife was not a fashion model, but a last-year law student at a college in Virginia where they live.

I like all people who love horses, but the Alcaldes and I, over that first slow drink under the Spanish sun, soon became fast friends. In describing outstanding horse people in this book the word "passion" is used again and again; and yet, there is no better word to sum up the feeling that persons like Hector and Karen have for horses, in this case especially Andalusians.

After that Sunday there followed a series of days in which I found myself together with Hector and Karen as they drove around southern Spain looking for the best Andalusian horses they could find and acquire for their farm in Virginia. All persons who go to exotic foreign places, like Lady Ann Blunt and the Alcaldes, are actually treasure hunters. And it was my good fortune to be caught up in their enthusiasm as they traveled from farm to farm, never knowing what to expect, but with the hope of finding some rare and precious equine gem.

Toward the end of their stay in Sevilla, Hector and Karen came to dinner at my ranch, Cañada Grande, after which, as we sat on the terrace, I heard more about their passionate quest for Andalusians. Hector's beginnings were not too unlike those of many horse lovers: "A good friend of mine had a Quarter-horse farm near Tampa, where I learned to ride on weekends. In a large lake on the property we'd often take the horses swimming, and during one of these outings it occurred to me just how individual animals differed in character and personality from one to another. I found this fascinating."

As Hector continued his story, the owls were beginning to call in the oak groves around us and somewhere off in the distance a fighting bull lifted its head to roar at the moon. "In 1962, when I moved to Virginia, I built a home and a small stable on a plot of land where I kept Quarter horses and Thoroughbreds, strictly for pleasure. Happily, my three children all grew up with horses and became accomplished riders.

"In the 1970's I became involved with racing Thoroughbreds and, along with a friend, retained a trainer and started claiming horses at The Charles Town Track in West Virginia. While I loved the animals and the sport, during the three years I was involved with racing, I always felt there was something else waiting for me in the horse world."

As Hector now spoke his eyes sparkled and his normally vigorous voice became even more so. "Gradually it seemed to me that I would really enjoy, more than sporting horses, breeding them. And as I traveled abroad and read more and more, increasing my general knowledge, one breed appealed to me more than any other—the Andalusian.''

So here was a modern man who, like James Michener, was not only an aficionado of Velázquez, but who, like the painter, had also been seduced by the beauty of Spanish horses. "Through my good friend, former Ambassador Alejandro Orfila," continued Hector, "I purchased my first Andalusian stallion, Fandango, a horse that I truly love and ride on a regular basis. Fandango is now seven and has been and is high-school-trained by Holly Van Borst.

"My dream to breed Andalusians came true when Karen and I purchased Takaro, our eighty-five-acre farm in the most beautiful country you can imagine, near Middleburg. I decided to build all my own facilities for the sole purpose of breeding, training, and promoting Andalusian horses. With our recently completed stables, indoor riding arena, tenant house, and turn-out sheds for the mares and foals, we can accommodate from forty to fifty horses." Hector then gestured to his wife. "Now Karen's playing a larger role with the horses. We've become interested in driving, and she's doing very well. In fact, we're currently involved in training our horses for it. Just to see one of these beautiful stallions hitched with its long mane flying and eye-catching action should interest people in America."

By the time the moon had traveled through the leaves of one giant oak tree and was peeking through the branches of another, Hector finished his story of infatuation with Andalusians: "Robert, I love these horses so much, and I'll do anything to try and make people in America appreciate them. Presently I'm in the process of developing my own traveling Andalusian show. This show would consist of approximately six high-schooled stallions and geldings that can perform in a manner similar to that of the horses of both the Spanish Riding School of Vienna and of Jerez de la Frontera. This project is just in the planning stage, but through it, if Americans are unable to come to our ranch to see Andalusians, we'll take the horses to them."

A half hour later as I watched the car carrying the Alcaldes disappear down the drive, its red tail lights becoming smaller and smaller, I was reminded how Velázquez through his paintings had brought the beauty of the Andalusian horse to the multitudes of tourists, among them thousands of Americans who annually visit Madrid's Prado Museum. And here, Hector Alcalde was taking the horses themselves to America to share their beauty—in the flesh—with his countrymen. As I heard the last gate slam shut, which indicated that the Alcaldes' car had left the ranch and was now turning onto the highway, I felt a rush of pride in my new friends and a feeling of contentment that this splendid breed of horse would be in such good hands in my own country.

DEEDIE WRIGLEY

"SOME ENCHANTED EVENING . . ." would begin the description of my first meeting with Deedie Wrigley.

The time was five or six years ago. The place was an art gallery in Scottsdale, Arizona, on opening night of an exhibition of photographs from *Equus* and *Stallion of a Dream*. The gallery was packed, tinkling with conversation and champagne glasses, when I looked across that crowded room and saw a woman whose physical attractiveness alone distinguished her from everyone present, and whose assured and natural manner radiated warmth and vibrations so positive that I left the people with whom I was talking and, not wanting to miss knowing her, walked across the room and introduced myself. That charismatic lady was Deedie Wrigley, accompanied by her strikingly beautiful daughter Misdee. Everything that I thereafter experienced and learned about Deedie Wrigley—lady and horsewoman—was extraordinary.

First, I beg to differ with the Webster which defines a "lady" as a woman of refinement; a definition that falls drastically short—too many women wrap themselves in the trappings of refinement, yet remain common as the vast majority when stripped of the disguise.

A True Lady remains such whether she finds herself in a cold, damp duck blind before dawn, or whirling around the dance floor at the White House.

A True Lady has modesty in the face of flattery, quiet courage in the face of adversity, selflessness in the face of need. She has a quick wit, a gentle touch, a kindness for all. She is a woman of the World and a child of Nature, and she is very rare.

Deedie Wrigley is a True Lady.

The daughter of Philip and Helen Wrigley, Deedie was raised in a world of silk ball gowns and silver tea services. But she was always comfortable, even more content, with blue jeans and canteens. Animals have always been an integral part of her life. From her youngest years she had pets ranging from white mice to wild goats. An experienced hunter, she gained a deep respect for the instinct and behavior of wild animals. But the one species that has remained most special to her, even guided the course of her life, is the horse.

Deedie Wrigley's involvement with horses began when she was a small girl on Catalina Island, where her family spent several months of the year. There, on their ranch, Deedie's happiest hours were spent racing across the rugged island terrain. When Philip and Helen Wrigley's interest was sparked by the Arabian horse, Deedie found a kindred spirit in the equine world.

From her father, Deedie learned to appreciate the Arabian as a "doing horse"—used for roping wild goats and moving island cattle to be shipped to the mainland. And it was from her mother that she learned to study the genealogy of the Arabian, tracing specific desirable characteristics to certain pedigrees.

Through the years, Deedie has developed the philosophy of breeding "beautiful athletes," horses who, not unlike herself, were as equally adept at performing in the show ring, where beauty and manners are paramount, as they were performing on the ranch, where intelligence and durability are demanded. And it was she, of course, who put her horses through the test. A normal course of events was for her to take her horse to a show, win all the prizes, and hurry home to ride the same animal on a roundup.

In 1969, Deedie Wrigley began to breed Arabians as a full-time business, which for her is a labor of love. Each horse on the farm is a special friend; each knows her step and her voice, often with a gentle nicker anticipating her approach and the carrot she brings, or the gratifying scratch on the withers she gives. It is this special rapport with horses that in part causes Deedie to be successful in her business. She appreciates and understands the animal's dignity and nobility and is conscious of its comfort and needs.

Both of her daughters, Helen and Misdee, could literally ride before they could walk; and like their energetic mother—billed by them as "the world's best"—their earliest childhood friends had four hooves, a mane, and a tail. It is Deedie's rapport with equines that her daughters say is the most special gift she could have given them. Helen, the elder, is not involved in the horse business, but is an excellent equestrienne. She shares a joie de vivre with her horses, and can coax the most skittish animal into the roaring surf or down a precipitous incline through her confidence and communication.

Misdee, Deedie's younger daughter, now works with her mother in the business and grew up competing in the show ring where she has an astonishing record of wins. Misdee's extreme good looks, combined with the handsomeness of the farm's horses, makes seeing her in the ring a special treat for anyone with an eye for beauty.

Recently, when I asked Deedie which of her horses had had most importance in her life, her answer in itself was proof of this remarkable lady's life-long devotion to horses, spelled not simply with an "e" but with an "es."

"When you get to my age," she says, "and have been around horses *all* your life, it is difficult to choose a favorite." Deedie started with Snowball, an ex-circus pony who, with her astride, would often sit down or bow on the narrow mountainous Catalina Island trails. Then came Jimmy, an ex-rental horse that entered her life when she was six. Next was a black colt picked out from the wild island horses, who died when he was six. "I mourn him to this day," comments Deedie. Then came a "rambunctious Palomino mare" who broke Deedie's arm twice "but nonetheless was greatly loved." By the time she was eleven, Deedie had graduated to Arabians. Names of old friends come to mind: Kholey, Bakir, and Bint Kholameh, who

is now twenty-six and the dam of Deedie's internationally famous stallion, Kaborr.

"Speaking of Kaborr," she says, "if you add importance to emotional involvement, he will have to be *the* horse. Son of Naborr, who is one of the breed's most important sires, and of Bint Kholameh, who can be traced to all of my early-memory horses, he himself will be listed this year as a Sire of Significance.

"Somehow," she continues, "there would have to be a place for my favorite beloved gelding Tasamar. A purebred, he made up in talent what he lacked in type. We had a once-in-a-lifetime rapport. We traveled literally thousands of miles together. He was a cutting horse—one of the best. In the fifties and sixties I showed him in open competition, and he often beat the Quarter horses. He taught me more about cutting cattle and 'reading signs' than any human being ever did. When I rode him without a bridle, which I often did in exhibitions, he always outdid himself. He would toss his head and roll his eye back at me as if to say 'hang on' and then he would begin to work with exuberance."

The relationship of Deedie Wrigley to her horses today and those in the past is far more spiritual than physical; it is a deep love and respect and, most of all, understanding. There is nothing that Deedie, Helen, or Misdee wouldn't do for their horses, and nothing, I believe, that their horses wouldn't do for them.

MARTHA AND HENRY DUPONT

URING MY TRAVELS I have heard many horse sto-ries, but one stands out as being stronger and more lasting than any of the others. Six or so years ago I was in Sevilla when my agent, Gloria Loomis, phoned to say that Mrs. Henry E. I. duPont had been in touch with her about arranging a meeting the next time I was in America. Mrs. duPont wanted to discuss the possibility of my doing a book on America's first breed, Morgan horses.

The following spring, when I was in New York, Gloria and I lunched with Mr. and Mrs. Henry duPont, whom I found to be two of the most charming, intelligent, and all-around attractive horse-loving people I have ever encountered. Naturally beautiful, sincere, and articulate, Martha du-Pont's joy for the Morgans that she raises, trains, and shows radiated from her like the golden, fall light that slipped through the window of the Plaza Hotel where we lunched. As the duPonts told me of their horses and farm, what a delight it was to partake of the pleasure that horses have brought to their lives.

When the conversation turned to Martha's favorite animals and mine—those of most heart and beauty—she told a true story, one that centers on her Morgan stallion, Lord Appleton, that will forever be etched in my memory and the memories of all who hear it.

"Robert," she began, "speaking of beauty, can you imagine a stallion whose attractiveness was of such magnitude, a horse of such rare charisma and aesthetic perfection that its former owner would not allow anyone else to see and be witness to its brilliance? Because the owner's greatest pleasure in life was the overpowering beauty of his horse, he had an arena built especially for it with a state-of-the-art lighting and sound system. And in the evening the man would go to the arena and, as the lights played on the stallion and appropriate classical music sounded, a sole spectator would sit in the darkness of the empty building, delighting in the extraordinarily beautiful animal before him."

When Martha duPont concluded her story, I could feel the goose pimples on the back of my neck as her words clearly projected on my imagination that dark arena with its single spectator lost in the blackness, while the magnificent stallion pawed the ground and arched his neck or tossed his dark, full mane and forelock under the dramatic theatrical lighting as the deep sounds of Wagner swept around him.

The stallion of the story is *now* happily at Nemours, the duPonts' Morgan farm, surrounded by attention and love, especially that of Martha and Henry duPont, and viewed by the many visitors who have heard of his extraordinary beauty.

Of my favorite horse people, the very very special ones have a great compassion for and sensitivity to people, as well as to animals. Martha duPont is an outstanding example of this. Twenty-five years ago she founded the nonprofit agency Child, Incorporated, which cares for dependent and neglected children, among them runaways. This work has earned her a reputation beyond the State of Delaware as being an outspoken, determined, and effective activist for children's rights. The boards that she has served on and the agencies that she heads demonstrate her great concern for human beings too young and powerless to protect themselves.

Martha duPont, however, carries more than one flag and spearheads more than one crusade. If children's rights are her obsession, then the Morgan horse is her passion. She was the originator of The Morgan Horse Breeders' Association, of which she is currently president. She is director of the national breed organization, the American Morgan Horse Association; and president of the Morgan Horse Development Institute, a nonprofit organization which promotes the American Morgan horse internationally, funds research grants, and sponsors breeders' seminars and other related projects.

When I asked "Muffin" about her love for horses, especially Morgans, she replied, "I've been

involved with them all my life, starting to ride at the age of four. When I was a teenager, I had my first formal lessons, which were from an army colonel who was tough. I learned dressage as a training tool in the classical sense. Europeans are more advanced than Americans in the use of long lines as a training device on the ground. It was this instruction that was so valuable to me in my work with horses, because ground work, if executed properly, gives one sensitive contact with the horse. Correctly done, the body of the horse and that of the trainer work together—practically as one—with the trainer giving the lead.

"I went to study in Europe and began training steeplechase horses. However, I eventually married and, at an early age, had children (she is the mother of seven), which brought my training to an end." But Martha duPont's interest in horses by no means terminated there. She founded the Delaware Pony Club where part-time she instructed children. And then the Morgan horse came into the duPonts' life. "After having been involved in the breeding of Thoroughbreds, we got into Morgans about fifteen years ago," she says. "My fascination with the breed and its history was responsible for this involvement. I can't tell you how moved I was by this little American horse and his past. I truly felt I could do something for this wonderful breed. It was then that my husband and I established Nemours Morgan Farm in Greenville where we now have approximately seventy Morgans, producing about twenty foals a year."

Taking an active part in the farm, Henry du-Pont is now retired from business and spends a good deal of time with the Morgans. Both of his parents were active with horses, his mother with Welsh ponies and his father, who designed numerous racetracks in use today, with Thoroughbreds. His aunt was Marion duPont Scott, known as "the angel of steeplechasing." Henry duPont's special interest is in pleasure driving, something he frequently does with a four-in-hand of Morgans.

And so one of America's most respected families admirably works to preserve and make better known an animal that was so important to the founding of this country. "In these days," says Martha duPont, "when Americans are turning back to their roots, we must help make them aware of this powerful, beautiful, and versatile little horse that cleared the colonial landscape, settled the West, became the official Army horse until the 1940's, held the record as the fastest trotting horse for one hundred years before he was crossed with other breeds to create his competition. He is the same horse that fought in the Civil War, and in one battle was the only survivor among men and beasts. On the other hand, in the forties, when American soldiers were saving the Lippizaners in Europe, our army lined up thousands of Morgans and killed them with saline injections after which they painfully dropped into trenches and were buried. They were not needed anymore. We had the jeep! But still the Morgan survived, both here and in other countries, to give enjoyment to thousands of people."

Later that afternoon as I looked out of the window of a California-bound aircraft, I was again reminded what a big country America is and what wonderful pages of history had been written in the forests and mountains and plains over which we were passing. And it felt good to know that as long as there are people like Martha and Henry duPont, that wonderful, big-hearted little horse the Morgan will not only be a reminder of America's traditional equine past, but will continue to bring pleasure and beauty to its future.

VIVIENNE LUNDQUIST

THE ROLLING HILLS of the 186-acre ranch are quiet. The green is broken only by the pattern of miles of neat white fencing. At the entryway to the Meadow Springs ranch house stands a life-size monument in bronze to Seabiscuit—who needs no introduction. And yet this ranch is a living monument not only to another breed of horse, one that traces its immediate romantic ancestry to the discovery of America, but to a woman of a courage, determination, vitality, and beauty *extraordinaire*.

Vivienne Lundquist's dark doe eyes, flame-colored hair, and aerobics figure would better identify her as a film star, rather than a woman who, even with a large staff, single-handedly runs Meadow Springs Peruvian Paso Ranch. Though her vitality and good looks shine forth, it is Vivienne's passion for horses—to be exact for the Peruvian Paso—that burns with brilliance. It was my good fortune to photograph one of her horses, which Vivienne personally handled during the entire session.

After the photographs had been taken, Vivienne drove me to meet two of her champion stallions, Antares and Florentino. As their owner strode into the enclosures with the vitality that Vivienne seems to put into everything in life, the long-maned Peruvian horses stepped confidently and affectionately forward to meet her. Anyone who has been around horses could have immediately recognized the mutual respect between woman and stallions and the love and pride she felt for them. Few humans have that rare touch with animals and know the fine line between firmness and affection that ensures a relationship of mutual admiration and caring. Vivienne Lundquist is one of these persons.

As evening approached and the shadows lengthened while a chilly wind bent the trees outside, I sat in Vivienne's living room, waiting for her to bring us tea. The walls of the room were covered with silver and silk—trophies, plaques, ribbons—the show awards that provide an impressive testimony to the Peruvian Pasos and to the owner of Meadow Springs Ranch. How was it that this striking Englishwoman, though she had been "wild about horses" as a child in Great Britain, was now not only in California, but one of the most important breeders of Peruvian Paso horses in the world? When Vivienne entered the room with our tea, I asked her this question.

"Well," she said, thinking for a moment while she rested her head on the back of the couch and ran her fingers through her hair, "when I moved to California, I was living in Rolling Hills when a friend invited me to come by to see 'a really different-looking horse' that had just come from Peru. I went over and there was this stallion with a well-muscled large chest and front and an expressive noble head—the kind you might see on a bronze statue in some European park." As she told the story, Vivienne had a distant look in her eyes, obviously the joy in reliving what would become a treasured moment for her, one that would not only set her life on a new course, but one from which a noble breed of horse would reach new glories because of their future association.

Vivienne continued her story: "I got on that horse and started to ride him around the arena and, after going about ten steps, I was absolutely in shock because I never moved on his back! I saw those front legs flip out to the side as if he were swimming. I felt his rear legs driving under me. I felt his energy and power—and it was fantastically exciting! What a horse! I never got over the experience.

"Later, when I once again found the opportunity to ride, I located some breeders and bought my first Peruvian horse. I'd intended to get two geldings for pleasure riding, but I decided instead to buy some mares so that I could start breeding them."

That first thrill of finding a breed of horse and knowing that it was her dreamed-of animal has led Vivienne on an adventure that few people have traveled—from the grassy highlands of Peru to obtain the very best stock available in the world which, like the precious pure gold cargo of a Spanish galleon, would be transported to Meadow Springs Ranch to be meticulously cared for and nurtured.

When the word "care" is mentioned in relationship to horses, I think immediately of Vivienne. In every detail she applies this word to its fullest meaning in the personal attention she gives her horses. Before a mare is a glimmer in a stallion's eye, the potential product of that union is a spark in Vivienne's creative imagination. "Regarding a breeding program," she says, "I have a basic philosophy that centers around one premise, 'for each particular mare breed to the very best stallion—no matter who owns him.' You must not be 'barn blind' by using a stallion just because he's on your ranch. No one stallion is perfect for all mares ... what suits one may not necessarily complement another. You must analyze each mare objectively, and select the best stallion especially for her."

To ensure her breeding program, Vivienne has constructed at Meadow Springs a costly state-of-the-art artificial insemination laboratory that was designed and built with the guidance of Colorado State University. It was at C.S.U., under the supervision of my friend Dr. Bill Picket, that Vivienne obtained her artificial insemination technician credential.

Once a mare has been bred, Vivienne waits with anticipation. The five-stall foaling barn, one of the most impressive structures on the ranch, is equipped with heat lamps and closed-circuit television cameras in each stall. Two sets of monitors hook up in the main house with another set of individual monitors in an apartment adjoining the stalls, where staff members trade off four-hour shifts all night when a birth is expected.

After a mare has foaled, Vivienne spends as much time as possible with "her babies." However, the supreme moment, she says, is when those babies are grown and are prepared to be ridden, at which time they are ready to give joy to other people—the joy that Vivienne felt when she rode her first Peruvian Paso. "Anyone can ride a Paso," she says proudly, "even if he's never ridden before. Also, people with back problems or physical handicaps can ride Peruvians—even some who can't walk without supports can enjoy the freedom of riding this wonderful horse. While I love to breed and show them, it's riding one, like that first thrill I had years ago, that gives me the most pleasure."

As I left the warmness of the main house at Meadow Springs Ranch and passed Seabiscuit standing in bronze, I read part of the inscription carved in the base of the statue: "Courage, honesty ... intelligence, and understanding ... spiritual in quality." And I thought how those words also applied to the owner of the Peruvian Pasos that were then quietly grazing the surrounding green hillsides.

WILLIAM SHATNER

"I COULDN'T BELIEVE the beauty of the horse," my friend excitedly told me. "I had gone to that Del Mar horse show depressed and gloomy, and here I was brought back to life by the overpowering presence and power of that animal. And if the horse weren't enough, the man who was riding it was equally impressive. Together they were like something out of a Greek legend. Like Alexander and Bucephalus. You can imagine my astonishment when instead of announcing the rider to be a professional trainer, the loudspeakers boomed out he was a movie star."

That was my first indirect introduction to William Shatner, horseman and gentleman. Weeks later, when one morning Bill Shatner came pounding onto the training field where I stood at Carlsbad, California, the horse he rode was unlike any I had previously seen. It was an American Saddlebred, the combined aesthetics and power of which can only be described as extraordinary. The Saddlebred is an animal capable of executing five gaits, the most impressive of which for me is the rack, which is a trained gait, a trot in which the horse's leg action is such that the rider remains stationary—which was unlike anything I had ever seen except in the Peruvian Paso.

When Bill dismounted from his flaxen-maned charger, Time Machine, I asked him what it felt like to be part of such a creature. "I once asked if I could pilot a powerboat," replied Bill, "one of those jet-propelled ones that go one hundred thirty miles an hour over the waves. I wanted to experience the thrill of such velocity, and somehow I was allowed to do this though I didn't go anywhere near its maximum speed. I sat on the seat while under me was a jet engine that roared and thundered and took me for what felt like a death-bend ride. When I returned to the dock, I smiled at the guys and said, 'Now I know it isn't the speed, it's what's beneath you that's thrilling!' And I think of the horse in that mode, a horse that is speeding along, barely in control but in control—wild, passionate, powerful. The total effect is equal to the most stimulating sensual physical pleasure and excitement I've ever experienced."

I then asked Bill—on top of all of that power and beauty—what does it feel like to change speeds on five-gaited horses? "The great horses, like Time Machine," he replied," are intricate pieces of machinery. It's like changing gears in a Porsche, yet guided by your fingertips and the pressure of your calves is a twelve-hundred-pound animal that is as finely tuned as is any brilliant piece of machinery. When you *are* in control there's a tremendous feeling of being in control."

I then asked Bill, though he is involved with other breeds of horses, why he is most keenly interested in Saddlebreds. "The Saddlebred," he answered, "has the most beautiful lines of any horse. Its symmetry, majesty, and motion set it apart from any other horse. It doesn't run the fastest, it doesn't endure the longest, but it carries with it something very special. I remember the first one I ever saw—a two-year-old black colt. He was some distance away in the stable and when I caught a glimpse of him I was reminded of those words from *South Pacific*, 'Across a crowded room.' I saw an animal that was both proud, majestic, and passionate. And I looked at him, and he was looking at me from what seemed like a great height—Saddlebreds have such long necks and all horses because of their peculiar sight lift their heads when they watch something close, and that's what this animal did. I stared up at him and saw in life the great statues that I had seen as a kid in parks, and for me Sultan's Great Day was the reincarnation of all the beauty and majesty of horses that I had loved in my dreams." Today Bill Shatner can look at the beauty not only of other people's Saddlebreds but of those that he breeds, trains, and rides at Belle Reve, his Kentucky farm.

If my new friend had been so impressed by a static Saddlebred, I then asked him how he reacted when he saw them move. Thinking for a moment, he replied, "My most vivid impression of the movement of these horses was in a legendary competition between two of the greatest Saddlebreds that ever lived. Three years ago there was a competition between Imperator and Sky Watch in the five-gaited stake at Louisville that rivaled anything that had ever happened in its history. When Imperator came into the ring, the crowd rose to its feet as I did, cheering and yelling, for the sight of that horse evoked a response right from your stomach, a rush of air out of your mouth in awe of what we saw before us. And you thought this had to be the most beautiful horse in the world. But following Imperator came Sky Watch, which was even more beautiful. It seemed impossible that there could be another animal more magnificent and majestic, more alive with motion than the first one. But indeed Sky Watch was. I have attended many of the great sports events throughout the world—the Super Bowl, the World Series, the Olympics—but I have never seen an athletic event like that and I have never seen people so impassioned."

When I told Bill about my friend's reaction to having seen him ride at the Del Mar show, comparing him and his mount to Alexander and Bucephalus, he smiled. "Because they were also two of my heroes," he said, "one of the greatest thrills in my life was when I was asked to play Alexander in a film." He then told how he had trained, worked out for nine months weight-lifting, practicing with shield and sword, and studying with the great Hollywood horse trainer Glenn Randell, who later said Shatner has more natural ability as a horseman than anyone in Hollywood. "Those words," says Bill, "meant more to me than winning an Oscar."

By the time filming started, Bill had also read everything there was to read about Alexander, and he felt he "really knew the man." The black Saddlebred stallion that took the part of Bucephalus had to be ridden without a saddle, with Bill having to master jumping on its back with the grace of an athletic king. However, he says that the most touching moment for him during that intense experience was one when the director called him aside and said, "Bill, we've got a sound problem. Yesterday when you were cradling the head of that dying soldier and leaned forward, the leather of your chestpiece creaked. We've got to correct it."

"As we walked across that high plateau with the magnificent buttes of southern Utah behind us," continued Bill, "we could have been in Persia; the landscape was identical. There I was, away from the company with the horse at my side when I had a flash—Alexander on his night raids had used padding on the hooves of the horses to make them more silent—but apart from that he must have had another sound problem—his leather uniform must have also creaked. I then turned and said to the director, 'Let's not deal with the problem; let's accept it as Alexander must have done.' And in that instant history dissolved for me."

In the days which followed that first meeting with William Shatner, we spent more time together. I was able to appreciate further his sensitivity to animals one morning as, at the San Diego Wild Animal Park, I watched as he rode an elephant and stood calmly inches from the face of a snarling tigress. But the moment that I enjoyed most, perhaps, was when the Land Rover entered the Przewalski enclosure and Bill commented on the rare, primitive beauty of these Mongolian horses, which confirmed my own feelings for them.

However, if I were to pick one moment from that time together in February, I would choose a late afternoon on a high hill swirled as if by a brush fire with black clouds of rain that passed quickly to leave the sky arched in rainbows; of the sun sparkling in the distance on the Pacific Ocean; and of a gentle man, a man of strength and action mounted on a magnificent horse, crossing the crest of a ridge. Even though my reason said that it was William Shatner and Time Machine, imagination effortlessly changed the figures of man and beast into those of the King of Macedonia and the horse from which he had conquered most of the then known world.

In my first horse book, *Equus*, horses were treated as wild animals, not yet domesticated. Now, with the conclusion of *Equus Reined*, man and horse have been seen through the ages in a romantic association that is the "way it should be." Obviously, there is another side to most relationships, and horses are frequently as abused by human beings as they are loved by them. However, as long as equines have men and women like Hector and Karen Alcalde, Deedie Wrigley, Henry and Martha duPont, Vivienne Lundquist, and William Shatner at their side, then romance, beauty and excitement, fascination, magic, and compassion will be synonymous with "equus reined."

EQUUS REINED, THE FUTURE

IN THE WILD, the future of free-living equines is precarious. It is almost certain that the only true wild horse, the Przewalski, exists today only in zoos. Zebra and wild asses are continually being pushed toward extinction by encroaching civilization—ignorance, agriculture, and domestic ungulates being the greatest dangers. While survival of these animals is constantly being abused by threatening pressures, domestic equines are also frequently abused by lack of human understanding. Time after time in distant parts of the world, I see horses unjustly treated because human beings fail to try to understand even the most basic signs of equine communication.

Years ago, realizing that a tremendous abyss in communication existed between man and horse, I undertook a study that later became the book *Such Is the Real Nature of Horses*. Prompted by having just scratched the surface in equine primitive behavior in that work and by the many letters my publisher received from readers, I began to formulate plans for a much more in-depth, long-term study of primitive equine behavior. Through the interest and support of Hector and Karen Alcalde, Deedie Wrigley, Martha and Henry duPont, Vivienne Lundquist, and William Shatner, this project has become a reality. Five or six years may pass before findings are extensive enough to be published. Work begins this summer with a month in East Africa scrutinizing the social behavior of Plains Zebra, after which long periods of time will be spent in the marshes of the Camargue with free-living horses that I have already extensively studied, as well as with groups of Przewalskis that are kept in family situations.

It is my feeling and that of the patrons of this project that if man has reined equus, he must then take on the responsibility of trying to treat with dignity and understanding the creature that has served us more than any animal in the history of this planet.

THE PHOTOGRAPHS

Listed with the identification of each image are various bits of information that I encountered while researching this book. The photographs were taken with one Nikon F2 camera, two Nikon F3 cameras (with motor drives), one 50--300mm Nikkor zoom lens, and two Nikkor 105mm lenses. For the most part film used was 400 ASA Ektachrome. Because of his contribution to this project, I thank my laboratory partner Rick Fabares for his creativity and many long hours.

Page 7
WILD HORSE RUNNING

The image that perhaps expresses liberty more than any other to man is that of a horse running free. Several thousand years before the birth of Christ, before the horse was domesticated, man sought equines only for food and clothing. Near Lyons, alone, the bones of tens of thousands of horses have been found close to one prehistoric cave settlement. Interestingly, in France and in Switzerland, horsemeat is today still consumed by humans.

Since the first horse, Eohippus, appeared more than fifty million years ago, more than two hundred fifty different types of horses have lived on earth. From the ancestors of Eohippus, that small animal which was not much larger than a fox, man has developed more than sixty breeds of horses, each with its own specialty. However, though the trained behaviors that humans have imposed on the horse are exciting and beautiful to watch, still the splendor of a stallion running free is difficult to match.

Pages 8–11
MORGAN HORSES

Justin Morgan, the legendary progenitor of the Morgan horse breed, was born in Springfield, Massachusetts, in 1789, the same year George Washington became America's first President. The Morgan's ancestry shall forever remain a secret, but we do know that this animal was a mutation possessing the ability to transmit to his offspring characteristics unique to himself and, many generations later, the same characteristics predominate.

Justin Morgan was originally named "Figure" and later got his name from the man who first owned him, Justin Morgan. He lived for thirty-two years and produced many get, the most famous of which were his three sons: Sherman, Woodbury, and Bullrush. Today's Morgans descend from these three stallions and crosses among them.

The Morgan is the only registered breed of horse ever perpetuated by the United States government. In 1907, the U.S. Morgan Farm was established in Middlebury, Vermont, and operated by the Department of Agriculture. The purpose of the farm was to breed Morgans to produce stallions for remount stations at various points across the country.

The Morgan horse was used to develop such breeds as the Standardbred, the Saddlebred, the Quarter horse, and the Tennessee Walker. He has adjusted to changing times down through the years. At one period in history, the Morgan fell from popularity and almost from the horse world. Thanks to many loyal friends, however, the Morgan remains today one of the most versatile horses in America.

Pages 12–13
RUNNING HORSE

Today feral horses still roam free in North and South America, Spain, Australia, and several other parts of the world. However, it is almost certain that the only truly wild horse, the Przewalski, has been eliminated from its natural habitat.

Pages 14–21
PRZEWALSKI HORSES

When I first saw Przewalski horses at the San Diego Wild Animal Park, an air of immediate and excited recognition swept over me. Their short, stiff black manes, their husky forms, their lovely delicate tonal shades of brown fur, and their white-circled and black-mascaraed eyes mirrored the horses that I had seen in the prehistoric caves of Spain. Meanwhile, other persons on the spectator train at the animal park turned away, "Oh, those look like mules," and focused on what to them were the more spectacular African rhinos on the right side of the track.

Since that first face-to-face encounter, Przewalski horses have been among my equine favorites. Their primeval stamp has a subtle beauty which in its own way is relatively as impressive as that of the Andalusian or Arabian. The Przewalski of today in appearance seems to be identical to his Ice Age ancestors. This phenomenon of pureness and sameness seems explainable not only by the hostile environment of the horse's native habitat, but by the Przewalski's aggressive and natural aversion to horses of other breeds with which in the wild it may have refused to cross.

Joan Embery of the San Diego Zoo:

The Przewalski horse of Mongolia and China is the only truly wild horse that exists today. The existence of these horses was officially documented and recorded in 1881, when Colonel Nikolai Przewalski, a Polish officer in the Imperial Russian Army, who had explored the wastelands of northern China, sent the skin and skull of an unknown wild horse to [what is now known as] the Soviet Academy of Sciences in Leningrad, where it was stuffed and still stands. That speciman convinced zoologists of the presence of a species considered extinct, along with the other equine prototype, the tarpan.

Coupled with the spread of man and domestic animals into previously unoccupied areas, the unfortunate decline of the Przewalski horse dates from the acquisition of modern firearms by the Chinese and Mongolian hunters; with competition for grazing and water, only forbidding territory north of Tibet and Mongolia offered sanctuary.

The first Przewalski horses were captured for zoos using relays of riders on fresh horses that would chase a herd until a foal dropped from exhaustion. Domestic nursemares then accompanied the young Przewalskis to Europe. The mortality rate was high, but more than fifty of these Mongolian horses did survive and reached collec-

tions in Russia, Germany, and England. The United States received its first specimens when the Bronx Zoo imported a pair in 1902.

Although breeding went well for many years, the captive herds diminished, so that by the mid-1950's only four animals existed in North America, with no viable offspring. Many of the European collections were allowed to die out or were killed by bombs during World War II. By that time the gene pool was in a perilous state. Fortunately, while groups of animals in the Western World were on the decline, Munich and Prague maintained sizable herds, and it is from these collections that new American bloodlines were strengthened. Today, there are over five hundred of these rare Mongolian horses in zoos around the world (almost one hundred in the United States), with the world pedigree book kept at the Halle Prague Zoo.

Though Przewalski horses may have once been used as mounts by the Huns and Chinese, their wild dispositions undoubtedly made them less desirable than other horses.

The only person with whom I have spoken who has experienced training a Przewalski is Joan Embery. She comments:

The training hours I spent with Bosaga, the Przewalski mare, were unique. I found dealing with her that she became more tolerant in time, more accepting of being handled and controlled. I always had the feeling that whatever I accomplished was possible because she had allowed me to do what I did, and not because I had imposed my will on her. It would have been difficult to force her to do anything, because Przewalskis don't accept discipline the way domestic horses do. You can punish a Thoroughbred, for example, when it misbehaves, but if you discipline a wild equine, it retaliates or fights you, and can become aggressive and dangerous. If Bosaga didn't want to lead, often I simply waited and stood my ground and hoped that she would give in, because to discipline her would have created an even greater conflict—this seems to be true for all wild equines with which I have dealt. They have to be convinced that what you want them to do is easier than resisting, that they won't be hurt by it—mutual trust is absolutely an essential factor in working with them.

Pages 24–25
ANDALUSIAN STALLION

Upon the Spanish discovery of America, it is not difficult to imagine, seeing this white stallion, how in Indian eyes these animals seemed at first to be gods sent from the heavens.

Pages 26–27
EGYPTIAN ARABIAN STALLION

Few other natural marvels of the world can compare with the beauty of the sculpted look of this Egyptian stallion. Egyptian Arabians are generally more fine-boned, smaller, and more stylized in their appearance than are other Arabian horses. Several years ago in Scottsdale, Arizona, I had the pleasure of meeting Judith Forbes, an expert in these horses; and of their history she writes:

The arrival of the horse in Egypt has been connected by most Egyptologists with the invasions of the Hyskos, for it supposedly entered the Nile Valley about the time of their conquest. Since about 1580 B.C. the horse has played a vital role in Egyptian culture. The Old Testament is liberally sprinkled with references to Egyptian horses. Solomon sang, "I compare thee, my love, to a company of horses in Pharaoh's chariots." Indeed the early Egyptian steeds showed the type of the pure Arabian breed as it is known today. With the decline of the Egyptian empire and the advent of Islam, the Arabian breed came to the fore again through the Mameluke Sultans. Most famous among them were Kala'un and Sultan Barkuh, A.D. 1382, whose stud eventually numbered some 7,000 horses.

Mohammed Ali the Great (1769–1849), originator of modern Egypt's renaissance, also obtained excellent Arabian horses with the help of one of his sons, Ibrahim Pasha. The most famous and eccentric collector of them, however, was Abbas Pasha, Viceroy of Egypt (1848–1854). His horses

were said to rival those of King Solomon, and it is from Abba's collection that most of the present day Arabians in Egypt, America and England descend.

Pages 28–29
ANDALUSIAN STALLION

This horseman seems to be riding out of nineteenth-century Spain, yet scenes like this are not uncommon in Andalusia today. Perhaps the most elegant public display of horseflesh in the world takes place there each year at the April fair of Sevilla. During this week, from Tuesday until Sunday, in a single morning thousands of horses promenade the streets of the fairgrounds in a spectacle without parallel. The majority of these animals are stallions and mares, with few geldings, which testifies to the temperament of the Spanish horse as well as to the control of their riders. Costumes are all period, which makes the display even more colorful, and carriages pulled by teams of the country's finest stallions and mares add further grandiosity to the event.

Page 30
PERUVIAN PASO STALLION

The first time one sees a Peruvian Paso in action it is difficult not to be impressed by the horse's amazingly smooth gait. The modern-day Peruvian Paso is considered by his aficionados to be the smoothest riding horse on earth. The Peruvian's natural gait eliminates virtually all motion for the rider and allows the horse to glide forward without moving the back between the croup and the withers. The best of these horses are motionless in the saddle even at speeds up to twenty miles per hour. The gait of the Peruvian horse can be as slow as a walk or as fast as an extended trot or slow canter. Both the gait and flashy leg action are inherited.

The ancestors of the present-day Peruvian horse came from Spain and were of Andalusian, Friesian, Barb, and Spanish Jennet blood. In Peru, the naturally gaited Spanish horses were carefully bred to produce the purest link that the modern world has with the once populous, naturally gaited horses. For several centuries no outside blood has been introduced into Peruvian Pasos, and now every purebred Peruvian horse has the inherited four-beat lateral gait which is the trademark of the breed.

The Peruvians did not breed exclusively for gait. Disposition was equally important. In fact, the disposition of the Peruvian horse is one of his most appealing virtues. As a result of strict culling, the Peruvian horse is intelligent, tractable, and eager to please. However, he has retained the presence and arrogance of his hot-blooded ancestors, and the modern-day Peruvian horse is said to still travel "like a conqueror."

Pages 32–33
CARRIAGE AT SUNSET

It is impossible to determine exactly at which point in history the horse was transformed from being an animal that was solely loaded with human or material cargo into one that pulled a wheeled vehicle. Probably this occurred at the same time in distinct parts of the world; and there is some evidence of the Chinese using carts as far back as the fifteenth century B.C.

James Hewat, noted driving and riding instructor, writes in *The Encyclopedia of the Horse:*

> The earliest carriage in perfect condition to be found today is the State Chariot of Tutankhamen (1361–1352 B.C.) in the Cairo Museum. The Romans used many heavy four-wheeled wagons as well as their chariots, but these were not adopted by other nations. The first recorded carriage to be built in Great Britain was by William Rippon for the second Earl of Rutland in 1555. Rippon is also recorded as having supplied carriages to Mary Queen of Scots in 1556, and to Queen Elizabeth of England in 1564. The true age of horse-drawn vehicles can be said to have arrived in the eighteenth century.
>
> By the 1920's the use of the horse-drawn carriage was, apart from tradesmen's vehicles, fast disappearing, but interest in driving for pleasure began to revive about the middle 1950's. The founding of the British Driving Society in 1957 has done a great deal to encourage driving in Britain. Many people now collect and restore horse-drawn vehicles of all types. Several firms do extensive rebuilding, and even building from scratch, carriage painting and lining, sign writing and decorating vehicles in the manner of the old craftsmen.

Today, worldwide interest in driving is responsible for national and international competitions and performance trials, a good many of which are won by the Hungarians.

Pages 34–35
WOMAN AND ZEBRA

This Hartmann's zebra mare represents one of the few types of wild equines that today exist in the wild. Africa and Asia are the last stronghold of wild equines that have not been changed by man through selective breeding. The Mustangs of America and so-called "wild horses" of Australia, South America, and other parts of the world are feral, or animals that were once domestic and that have escaped to live in the wild. Though zebras appear quite different from Przewalski horses, the differences are only skin-deep since their skeletons are almost identical.

Although renowned equine painter George Stubbs is most well-known for his portraits of Thoroughbreds, my favorite of all of his work is a canvas of a zebra standing in the greenness of an English park.

Pages 36–37
QUADRILLE

At sunset this quadrille of Spanish riders on Andalusian stallions perform on a natural stage of far more beauty than anything man could construct. Colonel Alois Podhajsky, former director of the Spanish Riding School of Vienna, writes:

> Developed from military methods of schooling horse and rider to greater agility and suppleness, horse ballets and quadrillas on horseback became

favoured amusements at the royal courts from the sixteenth to the eighteenth century . . .

A classical quadrille is performed by four riders, or a number divisible by four, who execute simultaneously various exercises and figures timed to music. *Haute école* movements at the different paces and varying degrees of difficulty are composed into a dance, the evolutions of horses and riders often reflecting as in a mirror. The precise performance requires of horses and riders an equally high standard of training and uniformity of appearance.

Pages 38–39
ARAB FOAL

That the Arabian horse did reach the Western World and was carefully bred here is a tribute to a number of persons, but certainly few greater efforts were made than those of Lady Anne Blunt whose imported stock has since had immeasurable influence on the breed. For her, searching in the desert for fine Arabian horses was like treasure hunting. Though many mediocre horses were brought to her, now and then an animal of true brilliance would appear. At the time of her quests for the horses of the desert, travel was not easy, a factor that did not deter Lady Blunt who in 1878 wrote of an expedition to Syria:

All day long people have been bringing horses and mares for us to look at, for we have given out that we wish to exchange Tamarisk for something better, and a very interesting sight it has been.

She then continues with the description of various horses, none perfect, that are brought for her to study, concluding with:

But our chief delight was to follow, when Beteyen ibn Mershid, sheykh of the Gomussa, rode up to Mohammed Dukhi's tent to pay a visit. He had just purchased from one of his people the "bridle-half" of a three-year-old mare, an Abeyeh Sherrak, and was riding her home when he heard that we were at Mohammed Dukhi's tent. The mare is so much

more remarkable than the man, that I must describe her first. She is a dark bay, standing fifteen hands or over. Her head, the first point an Arab looks to, is a good one, though I have seen finer, but is correctly set on, and the *mitbakh*, or join of the head and neck, would give distinction to any profile. Her neck is light and well arched, the wither high, the shoulder well sloped, and the quarters so fine and powerful that it is impossible she should be otherwise than a very fast mare. Her length of limb above the hock is remarkable, as is that of the pastern. She carries her tail high, as all well-bred Arabians do, and there is a neatness and finish about every movement, which remind one of a fawn or a gazelle. We are all agreed that she is incomparably superior to anything we have seen here or elsewhere, and would be worth a king's ransom, if kings were still worth ransoming.

Pages 40–43
EDWARDIAN LADY AND ANDALUSIAN STALLION

In over fifteen years of being day after day with a great number of Spanish stallions, never did I encounter a dangerous or really bad-natured horse. That artists have been captivated by the Andalusian's long flowing manes and tails, their arched necks and noble heads and overall impression of masculinity, is not surprising.

Many theories have been put forward regarding the origins of this breed which at one time was the most desired horse in Europe.

Maurizio Bongianni and Concetta Mori write in *Horses of the World*:

Some experts maintain that it descends from Barbs and Arabs that were introduced into Spain in the eighth century at the time of the Moslem conquest and crossed time and again with native breeds. Others are convinced that it is a descendant of the *Equus ibericus* encountered by Julius Caesar's legions in Roman times. Here, the theory is that, in prehistoric times, this horse made its way across the isthmus which then linked Africa with Europe (the present day Straits of Gibraltar), crossing from

Spain into North Africa where, conversely, it developed as the Barb. Lastly, there are those who claim that it is descended from 2,000 Numidian mares that were shipped across the Mediterranean to Spain by the Carthaginian general, Hasdrubal. Of all these hypotheses the most likely would appear to be the first.

The Andalusian dominated horse breeding in Spain from the twelfth to the seventeenth century, and was only seriously rivaled by the Arab. On his second voyage across the Atlantic, Christopher Columbus included a number of Andalusian and Neapolitan horses in his cargo. Thus, in addition to their already considerable influence in Europe, these two breeds, the Neapolitan itself a descendant of the Andalusian, also contributed to the formation and development of almost all the American breeds.

Not only did its aesthetic beauty make the Andalusian the ideal companions in life and on canvas for kings and nobles, but they were also prized for high school work. The foundation stock for the Spanish Riding School of Vienna were those animals from which the institute takes its name. Presently Andalusians may be seen in Spain performing at the School of Equestrian Art under the direction of Alvaro Domeca at Jerez de la Frontera.

Today within the Andalusian breed the purest strain is that of the Carthusians which was preserved by the Carthusian monks. When heavy horses were brought to Spain from Naples, Denmark, and Holland to cross with the smaller but beautifully proportioned Andalusian mares in an attempt to reproduce larger animals, the Carthusian monks kept their herds of Andalusians pure in a program of careful selective breeding.

Page 45
AMERICAN SADDLEBRED

Kentucky was the origin of the American Saddlebred that was developed for use as a saddle and light draft horse on plantations. It was known as a family horse, since it not only carried riders on its back, but was also enlisted for pulling carriages and plows. Its ancestry includes the Morgan, the Narragansett Pacer, and the English Thoroughbred.

It is well-known and admired not only for its aesthetic conformation, but for its different gaits, which vary from three to five depending on its training. The walk, trot, and canter are the basic three gaits, while five-gaited horses are trained for and adept at two additional gaits: the "slow gait," or four-beat "stepping pace," and the "rack," which is a speedier version of the "stepping pace."

The tremendous impression of power communicated by the Saddlebred, coupled with its physical beauty, is a rare combination in the equine world. The horse's small head, noble face, kind but alert eyes, long and graceful muscular neck, sculpted body, tall legs, and plumed tail produce in the human viewer the kind of reaction that comes with seeing any great work of art, whether it be a painting or an animal.

The American Saddle Horse Breeder's Association, incorporated in 1891, has the five-generation pedigrees of about 140,000 horses, and registers approximately 4,000 foals a year.

Pages 46–47
ARABIAN STALLION

Although the Arabs, like all horse breeders, are prone on occasion to over-glorify or romanticize their animals, still stories of attachments to their stallions and mares must bear some truth. According to Arab legend we are told:

Nothing can exceed the attachment that exists between the Arabs and their steeds. The mare and her foal inhabit the same tent with the family, and are caressed by all. The body of the mare is frequently the pillow of her master, and more frequently of his children, who roll about upon her and the foal, without the least risk.

The kindness thus engendered, is returned by the mare in many of those situations when the life of the child of the desert depends only on the sagacity and swiftness of his faithful courser.

When the Arab falls wounded from his mare, she will immediately stand still, and neigh until assistance arrives. Should fatigue compel him to lie down to sleep in the desert, she watches over him, and arouses him at the approach of man or beast . . .

The poverty of the Arabs enables them to afford but scanty nourishment to their horses. Besides the dry aromatic herbage they may chance to pick up, the Arabian horse usually has but one or two meals in twenty-four hours. At night it receives a little water; and five or six pounds of barley or beans and a little straw . . . Very little water is given, as the Arabs conceive (and justly) that much liquid injures the horse's shape and affects his wind.

The colt is mounted after its second year, when the Arab on all other occasions so kind to his horse, puts it to a cruelly severe trial. The colt, or filly, is led out to be mounted for the first time; its master springs on its back, and rides at full speed for perhaps fifty miles, over sand and rock of the burning desert, without one moment's respite, and immediately after this if it will eat as if nothing happened, its purity of blood and staunchness are considered incontrovertible.

Pages 48–49
GIRL AND FOAL

The photographs on these pages illustrate not only the delightful attitudes of a foal at play, but also the ability of young animals to imprint on human beings. Unlike the dog, the horse is not born a domestic animal. Each generation must be reintroduced to man and be tamed by the instillation of confidence and security. It is interesting to observe how some human beings have a special feeling for animals, know where to touch them, places that feel good to the animal; know how to move around them and gain their confidence. Other persons, hard as they try, have little tact with animals and destroy confidence instead of nurturing it. Perhaps one of the most profound statements ever made about animals was by Karel Capek when he said, "A wild animal is an animal which has no faith. Domestication is simply a state of confidence."

The foal in this picture was bottle-raised by the girl who also played with him every afternoon. Play is an essential part of the development and

lives of young equines whether they be Thoroughbred foals in Kentucky or baby zebra in Africa.

Pages 50–51
QUARTER HORSE AND COWBOYS

The cowboy and the horse is not only one of the most graphically exploited chapters of equine history—it is one of the most fascinating. Anyone who has seen a good cutting horse work cannot fail to be impressed by the animal-to-animal contact between equine and bovine in which man seems to play a relatively small part. To witness it is like watching a good hunting dog work birds, or a cattle- or sheep-dog in action.

The best cutting horses are Quarter horses, not only because they have the physique and agility for working cattle, but because in varying degrees they possess "cow sense." Animals which are so inclined, even when riderless and turned loose in a corral with cattle, will frequently try to cut and herd them. These horses seem to love working cattle and have a real aptitude for it.

Benton Watson of the American Quarter Horse Association writes:

The American Quarter Horse was the first breed developed in the Americas, originating during the colonial era in the Carolinas and Virginia where match racing was the outdoor sport . . . These horses were seldom raced beyond 440 yards (400m), hence the name "quarter miler."

The uses of the Quarter Horse were manifold. As the white man moved west he took the Quarter Horse with him to help conquer and settle the continent. The breed survived time and change because it excelled in qualities which were of major importance to people in diverse occupations and geographical areas. It was early adopted as the greatest round-up and trail-driving horse they had seen, for it possesses inherent "cow sense."

"The opening up of the West brought in its wake ranching on immense areas where cattle were reared and raised," comments David Black. "These ranches required hands known as cowboys to care for the cattle, to prevent rustling and 181 wholesale stealing by the Indians and other ranchers, and to round up the herds. Originally this word cowboy had been used at the time of the War of Independence to defame those who supported King George III, but by the end of the Civil War the term was accepted as describing all those who helped on the ranches.''

Pages 52–53
COURBETTE

Another of the spectacular airs above the ground, here performed by a mounted Andalusian, is the *courbette*, in which the horse leaps several times on its hind legs without touching the ground with its forelegs. The *courbette* may also be performed not mounted, but in hand.

Page 54
WOMAN AND HORSE

Few nineteenth-century images are more romantic than those of beautiful women in Edwardian dress accompanied by horses, in this case an Andalusian stallion. Helping a lady in such a costume to mount her steed was a task complicated enough that in 1890 instructions for male assistants were printed in *Riding for Pupils:*

The man who is to help the lady should advance facing her and almost touching the horse's shoulder with his left arm. He should stoop down a little away from the horse till his left shoulder comes almost under the lady's right hand, which she now advances and lays on it. At the same time he slides his left foot forward between where she stands and the horse and makes a cradle between his knees of his two hands. Into this she places her left foot, and pressing a little on the saddle, and a good deal on his shoulder, says ''Now,'' and gives a slight hop up. He straightens his back and stands upright, raising the foot that is in his hands steadily and rapidly up till he feels, by the sudden turn of it and the relief of weight, that the lady is in the saddle. She is, however, not really in a riding position at all, but only sits on her horse as a man

might sit on a gate with both feet at the same side of it.

He does not let go the lady's foot altogether, but keeps the palm of his right hand under the sole of the boot, while, with the left, he adjusts the folds of the habit so that all the loose part hangs down in front and not a single fold is between the lady's right knee and saddle. As soon as this is done she turns a little, as she sits, towards the horse's head and lifts her right knee over the crutch. The habit fits smoothly, and nothing remains but for the man to fasten the strap that is beneath the skirt over her left foot and put the toe in the stirrup. He should be able to do this by feeling, without stooping himself or raising the skirt to see what he is about.

Page 55
SIDESADDLE

In this photograph, a Bavarian princess sidesaddle-rides an Andalusian stallion.

Before 1890 a riding instructor in the Imperial Russian Army wrote:

Except as regards the legs, a lady should sit on a saddle exactly like a man. For some time there has been talk of ladies riding astride, which practice would deprive her of all feminine grace, and would afford no useful result. The great want in a man's seat is firmness, which would be still more difficult for a woman to acquire if she rode in a man's saddle, because her thighs are rounder and weaker than those of a man. Discussion of this subject is therefore useless. Ladies who ride astride get such bad falls that they soon give up the practice.

It has been proposed that the ladies should sit on the right side of the saddle. English and American journals have dwelt on the bad effects of girls on only one side of the horse, and they have tried to make out that this practice caused curvature of the spine. As I judge only by practical observations, I cannot say how it would affect children of five or six years old; but as I have often taught beginners of twelve and thirteen years old, I can certify most positively that girls of that age have nothing to fear on that score.

PINTO HORSES

It is known that two of the horses that Cortés brought to America had broken-coat patterns. This type of horse, or Pinto, was later much prized by the American Indians, who selectively bred for them. It has been speculated that the mottled coat was partly desired because of the camouflaging effect, but also of strong appeal to the design-minded Indians must have been the interesting patterns of black-and-white or brown-and-white hair when compared to a solid-coated animal.

As has already been said in this book, the impact of the horse on the Indians of North America is immeasurable. Walter Prescott Webb writes in *The Great Plains:*

Then came the horse; and overnight, so to speak, the whole life and economy of the Plains Indians (of the United States) was changed. Steam and electricity have not wrought a greater revolution in the ways of civilized life than the horse did in the savage life of the plains. So important was the horse in the Plains culture that the anthropologists have named the period extending from 1540 to 1880 the horse culture period. Practically all that scholars know about the Plains Indians comes from that period. The pre-Columbian time is one of conjecture; the reservation period after 1880 is little else than a story of imprisonment. It has already been stated that the Plains Indians maintained their integrity against the white man much longer than any other group. It was the horse and the buffalo, but primarily the horse that enabled them to hold out; without the horse they would have been easily disposed of, but in possession of this animal they were both uncontrollable and formidable.

About the origin of the Indian's horses, Walter Prescott Webb says:

It is generally accepted by anthropologists that these herds originated from the horses lost or abandoned by de Soto about 1541. Whether they came from de Soto's horses, or from those of Coro-nado, or from other explorers is not material; we know that the Kiowa and the Missouri Indians were mounted by 1682; the Pawnee by 1700; the Comanche by 1714; the Plains Cree and Arikara by 1738; the Assiniboin, Crow and Mandan, Snake and Teton by 1742; and the most important tribe, the Sarsi, by 1784. How much earlier these Indians rode horses we do not know; but we can say that the dispersion of horses which began in 1541 was completed over the Plains area by 1784.

All the Plains Indians were good horsemen, but the Comanche Indians were certainly among the best, if not the very best of them all. Their position on the Southern Plains made them among the first to come into possession of the Spanish horses as they came out from Mexico and drifted northwards. The climate of the Southern Plains was the best climate for the horse. He could live and thrive there the year round. Since the south was the natural habitat of the wild horse, they soon became more numerous there than on the Northern Plains, and therefore the Comanches had more horses than the northern tribes. The contact of the Comanches with Mexico made it possible for them to recruit their herds by theft from the Mexicans. They in turn, supplied the neighboring tribes, with the result that horses were constantly moving northwards.

As a race of Indians, George Catlin, famous painter of the American West, found the Comanche on foot to be unattractive and awkward in their movements, though he added:

. . . but the moment they mount their horses, they seem at once metamorphosed, and surprise the spectator with the ease and elegance of their movements . . . the moment he lays hands on a horse, his face even becomes handsome, and he gracefully flies away like a different being.

In their ball plays and some other games they are far behind the Sioux and others of the northern tribes; but in racing horses and riding they are not equalled by any other Indians on the continent. Racing horses, it would seem, is a constant and almost incessant exercise, and their principal mode of gambling. . . .

Frozen in space, this Andalusian stallion, in the capriole, transmits an equine expression often depicted by sculptors and painters. It is not usual to see a capriole well executed, but when this does occur, an instant charged with excitement and beauty is experienced. Most often the horse does not leap high enough, or hold its body parallel to the ground, or extend hind legs to full capacity. But when all of these elements do come together, the spectator is indeed privileged to a rare moment of equine beauty.

Anthony Dent, leading authority on the history of the horse, and author of *The Horse: Through 50 Centuries of Civilization*, writes:

The Andalusian of medieval times was by definition a destrier or knight's charger, and inside the Iberian peninsula all knights bestrode an Andalusian or part-bred approximation thereto. Outside the Hispanic region, to the far end of the Mediterranean, the Andalusian was the destrier *de luxe*, commanding top prices from Normandy to Cyprus. William the Conqueror rode one at Hastings; nobody else in his army could afford one, or if they could cared to expose it to the hazards of a Channel crossing and the broad axes of the house-carls. Because conditions of warfare in days and land of the Cid Campeador differed greatly from those obtaining on the marches of the Frankish empire to the East, not least because the 'foul paynim' in the shape of the Moor was a light horseman but not primarily an archer, the Spanish hidalgo was less heavily armoured than his French or Bavarian counterpart and found it essential to preserve mobility faced with an enemy who put practically no infantry into the field and must be outridden if he were to be beaten at all. Not but what a noble Andalusian was quite capable of carrying all the armour that was later piled onto it.

Flat out these horses race at the tideline on the southern coast of Spain in a week of formal races that attract betting crowds. Although these jockeys wear formal silks and the animals they ride are Thoroughbreds, some of which are from England and Ireland, the scene gives one an idea of the races that centuries ago may have been held on this same beach by the Phoenicians and Romans.

Alexander Mackay-Smith, former editor of *The Weekly Chronicle of the Horse*, writes in his book *The Horse in Art and History*:

Horse racing has probably existed as a sport since men first mounted horses. It was popular in ancient Greece and draws the largest crowds of any sport in America today, where it is a big business. But from the Renaissance to the early twentieth century, horse racing deserved to be called the sport of kings, or at least of the nobility. Light horses called "hobbies" were bred in England and Ireland from the fourteenth through the sixteenth centuries, and Italian noblemen imported them in considerable numbers to compete in the principal cities of Italy.

None of the three horses from whom all modern Thoroughbreds trace their descent in the direct male line is known to have raced, comments Peter Willett, though one of them, the Beverly Turk, was said to have enabled his owner Colonel Beverly to escape capture at the Battle of Boyne (1690) by outpacing his pursuers. The other two founding fathers of the Thoroughbred were the Godolphin Arabian and the Darley Arabian. The Godolphin Arabian is believed to have been foaled at the Arabian stud of the Bey of Tunis in 1724. The Darley Arabian was the purest of the pure, as he was certified as being "of the most esteemed race among the Arabs both by sire and dam, and the name of the race is called Manicha." He was imported from Aleppo in 1704.

GIRL AND ANDALUSIAN STALLION

Few mysteries of animal-human relationship evoke more tenderness and passion than does that of women and horses. Part of the beauty of this association may be summed up in the line "strength by gentleness confined." Some years ago while doing the book *All Those Girls in Love with Horses*, I was time after time impressed by the young women I met and photographed all over the world, and of the high degree of accomplishment that each had attained in her particular equestrian activity.

Often I was told that women, being gentler and more patient than men, have more success with horses who respond to those qualities better than they do to force. Good horsewomen, however, naturally do know how and when to use a strong hand if discipline is needed.

SPANISH WOMAN AND HORSE

Writers have devoted more words to equines than to any other animal. The beauty of the horse, both ridden and free-running, has for centuries been a source of creative inspiration. In fact, one might question how many celebrated authors have not at one time or another used horses in their work. To many writers of books, horses are passionate creatures the mere thought of which fortunately brews up such strong images that they, as long as words are read or heard, will give pleasure to us and to the generations that follow us. Shakespeare, García Lorca, Faulkner, Byron, Steinbeck, Chaucer, Cervantes, Melville, and Xenophon are but a few of the authors to whom the horse has had special meaning.

LEVADE

This mounted Andalusian stallion performs the *levade* in which the horse should rise on its deeply bent haunches with its forelegs folded under its chest, while the other horse is doing the higher *pesade*. Andalusian stallions like these were taken to Vienna in the 1500s to serve as the foundation stock of the Spanish Riding School there. Anne Charlish tells us:

> In the art of dressage, however, the Spanish Riding School of Vienna is still believed by many to be the supreme achievement in control and discipline of the horse. The Renaissance courts of Europe produced three chief styles of classical equitation and there were the Spanish School of Vienna, the Portuguese of Marialba and the French, first at Versailles and then at Saumur. The Spanish and Portuguese favored a high degree of collection and control, while the French approved a lighter, high-stepping, more showy style. At the same time, the Swedish and German styles were followed in those countries with their greater emphasis on discipline, rein control and leg aids, their proponents considering that the horse above all must be obedient and that the innate intelligence could not be assumed. All these styles existed chiefly for teaching cavalry officers to ride—none more so than the Spanish School of Vienna, which was established by 1572. Andalusians were considered at that time to be the most desirable breed in Europe, and so it was the Spanish horse and the Spanish style of riding that were offered to the Austrian cavalry.

LEVADE

The facial expression of this Andalusian stallion doing a *levade* is familiar to anyone who has ever visited Madrid's Prado Museum and enjoyed its Velázquez collection. When I first arrived in Spain in 1958, every Sunday I would walk across the street from the pension where I was staying to spend the morning with the paintings of Goya and Velázquez at the Prado. The Andalusians that prance, parade, and rear on Velázquez's canvases are identical to those that I would later know when in the spring of 1959 I went to live in Sevilla (birthplace of Velázquez), which has been my home ever since.

Used as work animals on fighting bull ranches, Andalusians are today very much a part of Spanish country life. Often when I ride my own white Spanish stallion around my ranch and see vaqueros working cattle across the road at the fighting bull farm of Juan Pedro Domecq, except for their manner of dress, they could be characters out of Goya's *Tauromaquia* series of etchings. Like Velázquez, Goya also used the thick-necked, heavy-chested, long-maned Andalusians in his paintings.

Pages 72–73
ARAB STALLION

Today in a world of computer, equine-breeding programs and pedigrees one might wonder just how the Arabs kept record of their animals and maintained the purity of their blood. Anthony Dent, author of *The Horse: Through 50 Centuries of Civilization*, tells us:

The greatest care is exercised in breeding kohlan, or Kaillian, the noble race; much ceremony takes place as well at the union of these animals as at the birth of a foal; and a certificate is made out properly authenticated, within seven days after the event. It is generally believed that pedigrees of the noble race of horses exist of not less than five hundred years, with sire and dam distinctly traced. The following pedigree is mentioned by Weston, in his Fragments of Oriental Literature; it was found hanging round the neck of an Arabian horse purchased by Colonel Ainslie, during the last campaign in Egypt against the French.

"In the name of God, the merciful and compassionate, and Seyd Mohammed, agent of the High God, and of the companions of Mohammed and of Jerusalem, Praised by the Lord, the omnipotent Creator. This is a high bred horse, and its colt's tooth is here in a bag about his neck, with his pedigree, and of undoubted authority, such as no infidel can refuse to believe. He is the son of Rabbaing, out of the dam Lahadah, and equal in power to his sire, of the tribe of Zazhalah. He is finely molded, and made for running like an ostrich, and great in his stroke, covering much ground. In the honours of relationship he reclaims Zaluah, sire of Mohot, sire of Kollach, and the unique Alhet, sire of Mansseth, sire of Alshek, father of the race down to the famous horse the sire of Lakalala; and to him be ever abundance of green meat, and corn and water of life, as a reward from the tribe of Zazhalah, for the fire of his cover, and may a thousand branches shade his carcase from the hyena of the tomb, from the howling wolf of the desert; and let the tribe of Zazhalah present him with a festival within an enclosure of walls; and let thousands assemble at the rising of the sun, in troops, hastily, where the tribe holds up, under a canopy of celestial signs, within walls, the saddle with the name and family of the prossessor. Then let them strike the hands with a loud noise incessantly, and pray God for immunity for the tribe of Zoab, the inspired tribe."

Pages 74–75
CAPRIOLE

This Andalusian stallion and its rider seem to be literally sailing through the sunset sky, which brings to mind one of the most famous equine legends of all time, that of Pegasus the flying horse.

Pegasus was the winged-stallion offspring of Medusa, the gorgon, and of the sea-god, Poseidon; and was born at the springs (*pegoe*) of ocean from which he got his name. On his birth he soared into the air and made his first landing where the acropolis at Corinth stands. While he was drinking from a fountain he was captured with a golden bridle and tamed by the Greek hero Bellerophon who later rode him off to kill the chimera. The river of Muses known as Hippocrene sprang from one of Pegasus' hoofprints on Mount Helicon. The image of the winged horse appears on many early coins of Corinth.

Pages 76–77
WOMAN AND LUSITANO STALLION

If Paul Revere's ride is the most famous male mounted sojourn across the countryside, then his female counterpart is, without a doubt, Lady Godiva. Anthony Dent, an authority on the history of the horse, tells us:

No English pageant is complete without a representation of Lady Godiva; even in places far remote from Coventry, where the legend survived long enough to be committed to writing. As a slice of history the story of the wife of the cruel earl who said he would repeal his unjust taxes only if she rode naked through the streets of Coventry is the most effective turn on the hill, streets ahead of Alfred and the Cakes, well up in the Robin Hood bracket. And like Robin, Godiva is a figure of mythology, not of history. Only her personality has been grafted onto the historical Godiva, Lady of Mercia, aunt of Hareward the Wake, perfectly authentic, identified and described in quite prosaic documents; the wife of Earl Leofric, who was not at all the monster of rapacity painted by the legend. An explanation must be sought in pagan tradition, either in the deep layers of Celtic myth along with Epona, the patron goddess of horses, or at the level of Anglo-Saxon heathendom with its sacred horses figured in the arms of Brunswick and Kent alike, but more probably in the revival of heathendom which the Viking invasion brought to England.

Pages 78–79
JOUSTING

Even in modern-day exhibitions, tournament participants are frequently injured in jousting matches. Presently, there are jousting associations in a number of countries that compete annually in international tournaments. Monique Dossenbach writes in *The Noble Horse:*

The question as to whether the French or the Germans invented the tournament is just as hotly debated as whether a tournament horse was or was not a carefully trained, well-ridden animal.

It was a Frenchman, Geoffrey de Pruelly, a knight himself, who was killed in a tournament in 1066, who provided the first written tournament rules.

In principal a tournament was defined as follows: two riders rode towards each other on parallel tracks, separated by a waist-high barrier, and, using long lances, tried to lift their opponents out of the saddle. It was, therefore, an advantage to have a deep saddle which provided a more secure seat. It was not necessary to be an adept rider, as the horse quickly learns to move forward at its heavy gallop, but courage was certainly a prerequisite.

Tournaments were always dangerous affairs, even in de Pruelly's time when full suits of armour were still unknown. Even a blunt lance could cause a lethal wound, and a fall was equally risky to a rider whose mobility was so restricted.

Many of the various forms of tournaments were exceptionally dangerous. In 1241 at one single tournament, for example, held in Neurs in the Lower Rhine region, no less than sixty knights were killed, a large number said to have "been asphyxiated in the dust or trampled to death by horses."

Pages 80–81
JOUSTING

One of the most romantic and flamboyant periods of equine history was that of chivalry and the tournament. Few sights can match that of brightly costumed horses with riders dressed in armor and matching colors, lances extended, pounding full speed at one another backgrounded by the subtle green of the English countryside.

Charles Chenevix-Trench, author of *The History of Horsemanship*, among other books, writes:

The focus of chivalry was the mounted knight. During the eleventh and twelfth centuries, when the cult was developing in Europe, he was immeasurably superior to the foot soldier that he could look on war as a game, played for honour and profit. When no war was available, both could be won with less trouble and discomfort in tournaments. With these was linked the pursuit of "courtly love," or polite adultery. A knight selected some married lady, preferably of a rank slightly higher than his own, and by prowess in tournament won her amatory favours. Not unnaturally, the Church disapproved of tournaments, but could not stop them.

The earliest tournaments were savage little

battles, with sharpened weapons, between gangs of knights more or less equal in numbers. Gradually these became single combats, more and more formalized, with strict rules such as a ban in striking an opponent's horse. There was a regular class of "knight errant," perambulating tournament experts who made a good profit from the horses and the defeated knights.

Late in the thirteenth century the English longbow made its dramatic appearance, the archer, not the knight, became master of the battlefield. Because horses could not ride through the arrow hail, knights, encased in heavier and heavier plate armour, had perforce to fight on foot. Only in the tournament did the ideal of chivalry, the mounted knight survive.

Page 82
THE HUNT—GREVY'S ZEBRA

Hunted in prehistory by cavemen, the zebra is one of the few equines upon which man still preys. In Africa, not only does the zebra continue to be a source of nourishment to indigenous peoples, but it is still, as it was in the Stone Age, hunted for its attractive skin.

Joan Embery says:

The Grevy's zebra, also highly endangered, are the largest and most stunning of the three types of zebra. They have narrow stripes, large, rounded ears, and a broad dorsal stripe bordered by white. Found in the desert-fringe areas of Northern Kenya, Southern Ethiopia, and in three isolated parts of Somalia, they number only a few thousand. Although hunting and poaching have affected all zebras, the Grevy's, with its vivid narrow stripes, has been particularly valued for its skin. . . .

Grevy's zebra, having the longest splint of bones of any member of the horse family, are thought possibly to be the most primitive living equines. It has also been speculated that the earliest equids were spotted and striped and did not have solid coloration. The Grevy's narrow stripes are regarded as the most ancient coat patterns among living equines, while the zebras that evolved later had fewer and broader stripes. Grevy's zebras do not

form permanent bonds, as do other species of zebra. Herds constantly change and solitary stallions are often territorial. This may represent the original form of social organization among equids, for Eohippus is presumed to have been territorial.

Page 83
PLAINS ZEBRA FOAL

Joan Embery:

Though all zebras look alike to most people, there are three primary types: plains zebra, mountain zebra, and Grevy's zebras. Each has a different striping pattern and comes from a different range, though in some areas ranges overlap. The most widespread and numerous are the plains (or common) zebras, so called because of the type of terrain in which they are found in East and Central Africa. Although their numbers have dropped in recent years, an estimated 300,000 roam the plains and savannahs from Southern Sudan to North South Africa. These zebras have shorter heads, smaller ears, and are more ponylike (13.2 hands) than their relatives.

Each zebra's stripe pattern is as unique as are individual fingerprints in humans. It's hard to imagine that this vivid stripe pattern also serves as a type of camouflage. At a distance the stripes help to break the zebra's outline, blending it with the background. Stripes can also be deceptive in herd situations, when zebra are tightly bunched. In the blur of movement, individuals are almost impossible to distinguish.

Though there are few trained zebras, I am sure there have been many more attempts than successes. I have heard stories by horse trainers of some wild zebra rides, most of which ended abruptly, never to be tried again. Exceptions to the rule are usually found in the circus. At Circus World, in Florida, there are two zebras trained to pull a chariot. I spoke with their trainer, who explained that he had always worked them together as a pair. Singly they were difficult to control. Most trained zebras have been common zebra, since the other species are endangered and to obtain and keep them requires special permits.

Pages 84–85
HARTMANN'S ZEBRA WITH WOMAN

Joan Embery:

Mountain zebras inhabit the mountain ranges of Southern Africa. They are small donkey-like animals that stand no more than twelve hands at the withers. Mountain zebras, like plains zebra, have broad stripes, but their bellies are white. They have a flap of skin, called a dewlap, on the underside of their necks, and horizontal bars in the pattern of a gridiron (football field) on their croup. There are two types of mountain zebra: the Hartmann's and the Cape. The Hartmann's are larger and their stripes are more widely spaced. Like the plains zebra, mountain zebra live in small herds. Often, groups mingle, graze together for a time, then move off, each band in its own direction. They are nonterritorial, nomadic, and migrate often. A herd stallion stands guard over five to fifteen mares and foals. Young stallions and those without herds of their own form bachelor herds. A dominance hierarchy exists within the family groups. The herd provides safety to individuals from predators such as hyenas, lions, and hunting dogs. Yet, man is the greatest threat. During the last twenty years Hartmann's mountain zebra have dropped alarmingly, from more than fifty thousand to fewer than five thousand, mainly due to competition with domestic livestock for food and water.

Zebras are resistant to common African diseases that affect horses. Therefore, efforts were made by government and private agencies to train them and cross them with horses and donkeys. However, because they were as resistant to training as they were to disease, these programs did not prove successful.

Pages 86–87
ARAB TROUPS

Though Arab descriptions of treatment of their horses have been accused of being exaggerated, Carl Raswan, who lived among the Bedouins and is the author of *Drinkers of the Wind,* offers this firsthand experience:

With surprise I observed that Ghazal [a stallion] was not hobbled but walked freely about. I asked the sheykh if the stallion would not disturb the mare and her foal, and would not run off into the desert?

Ghazal, the Bedouin assured me, knew what was expected of him as a member of the family. However, another owner and new environment might make a difficult horse of him . . .

The old man continued by telling me that he had met with no difficulty teaching Ghazal the meaning of thirty-seven words. "Ghazal's understanding mind," he added, "has also learned many signs of my hands and eyes."

Urged on by my interest, the sheykh offered to show me still another example of Ghazal's intelligence.

As we walked away from the tent, Ghazal's head was at once attentively directed to his master.

The sheykh asked me to stay behind while he approached my own horse. Suddenly the old man stumbled—purposely, of course—and threw himself full length upon the ground.

Ghazal snorted in fright. He wheeled about and raced full speed toward the prostrate form of his master; there he pawed the ground and neighed loudly as if calling to him. But when the sheykh did not answer, Ghazal began to turn the man's body over cautiously with one of his hoofs.

Ghazal nipped at Sheykh Ammer with anxious little caresses. Then the stallion tossed his head and neighed tremulously. "Ghazal!" whispered the sheykh.

At once the horse sought the ground, his muzzle close to the man's face.

"Naum—sleep!" the sheykh said.

With a little moan Ghazal went down on his forelegs, bent his hocks and settled upon the sand, rolling over on his side and stretching his limbs.

The sheykh crawled across Ghazal's withers, seated himself upon his back.

"Groom—arise!" he called.

With no apparent strain Ghazal lifted his body to a kneeling position, then rose to his haunches to stand firmly on his feet.

STALLION OF THE SEA

This Andalusian stallion and his grooms appear to have stepped out of a nineteenth-century romantic painting of *I Barberi*. American horsewoman Lida Fleitmann Bloodgood tells us:

These riderless races, run annually for centuries during the Roman carnival, were known as *I Barberi* because the horses were chiefly Barbs or Arabs. The horses, entirely loose, wore only a network of pear-shaped goads on their flanks and their owners' colours in head-plumes. Starting at Piazza del Popolo, where they were released by colorfully attired attendants called *barbaresche,* they galloped down the Corso between cheering crowds until stopped by a sheet drawn across a now non-existent street near the Piazza Venezia.

Introduced to Rome by Venetian Pope Paul II in the fifteenth century, the races were run less for monetary reasons than for the honour of winning the *pali*, a silk banner similar to those from which the famous Palio of Siena derives its name. At first popular only among the masses, during the eighteenth and nineteenth centuries the races became fashionable among the aristocracy, and Roman princes spent fortunes on breeding horses branded with their heraldic crests for these races. In 1882 the races were prohibited by royal decree after a fatal accident among the crowd occurred under the eyes of Queen Margherita, who was watching from a balcony of Palazza Fiano. They were continued for a short while in the Piazza del Popolo, enclosed by hoardings, and later in the Piazza di Siena, but eventually died out.

These races served as inspiration for Vernet, Goethe, and Géricault. In turn Géricault was of tremendous influence on his friend Eugène Delacroix to whom he wrote that it was "absolutely imperative to study horses" even to the extent of practically living in the stables from dawn to dusk. In 1832 Delacroix was sent as part of a diplomatic mission to the Sultan of Morocco, after which North African horses and their handlers and riders became one of his favorite subjects. Among the most well-known of his horse paintings is "Horses Emerging from the Sea," which was done in 1860, just three years before his death at the age of sixty-five. Michael Seth-Smith, noted equine writer, comments about the painting:

It epitomizes the romantic idea of which the horse is so often the symbol. The rider, intertwined in the curving necks of the two magnificent steeds rearing up out of the waves, echoes Delacroix's experiences in Morocco some thirty years before . . . The horse was a recurring image throughout his career. He produced at least eleven major works on the subject between 1822 and 1860.

The horse from the beginning of recorded legend has been associated with the sea, which in its power and strength and foam provide the chargers for Neptune's cart. Perhaps the most famous steed in literature is Pegasus, who was the offspring of the sea-god, Poseidon. Anyone who has seen horses in the surf can imagine from where these myths spring, as curved necks of stallions with wind-whipped snowy manes seem kindred to the arch and crest of the powerful waves with their white froth and spray.

ANDALUSIAN MARE

This mare and her companion both have Moorish ancestry. While most Andalusians are born black or dark in color and with age turn gray and eventually white, bay is a recognized color as is black (although very few pure black animals exist). Perhaps one of the most famous of all Spanish horses was a black charger called Morzillo which in 1524 was ridden by Hernán Cortés as he left Yucatan and headed south towards Honduras. Grant Uden writes in *High Horses*:

It was a difficult expedition. His forces had to thrust through hostile country . . . Fodder for the horses was scanty and they were reduced to poor condition, Morzillo among them.

The final piece of bad luck for the black charger came when he ran a splinter into his forefoot and was badly lamed. To ride him further would have been the height of cruelty, but the expedition could not be delayed. Cortés therefore placed the Black One in the charge of an Indian chief, making it very clear that he was a most precious animal and that he must be thoroughly cared for until someone was able to return for him.

The cavalcade moved on, and the Indians were left with the prized possession of the god-like general. Anxiously they made the best arrangements they could. Morzillo was given his own attendants, housed in a temple and fed on specially prepared food. But the black horse wanted, not luxury but simple veterinary knowledge and skill in a country that had none. The conquestador's horse grew gradually weaker and died, amid the lamentations of the frightened chief and his people.

They had failed the Spanish god, the descendant of the sun, and when he returned to claim his own they would not be able to produce him. Only one thing could be done. They could make a model of the horse and pay it the honour that was due. So, in place of the living animal, they carved a curious likeness in stone and, in time, came to rank it with the high gods of the Mayas.

Neither Hernán Cortés nor any of his men came back to recover the foundered horse. In time fear was forgotten, but not the fame and power of Morzillo, set majestically if incongruously, with the rain-god Chac, with the pendulous nose, and the fearsome feathered serpent Kulkulcan.

Page 95
CAPRIOLE IN HAND

The airs above the ground, of which the capriole is the most spectacular, are (except for the *levade* which at this time had not been perfected) precisely described in the 1730 *École de Cavalerie*:

All the airs are so called which the horse leaves the ground more than he does in the terre-à-terre. There are seven of them, as follows: the Pesade, the Mézair, the Courbette, the Croupade, the Balotade, the Capriole, the Step and Leap.

Pesade. This is an air in which the horse lifts the forehand off the ground in one spot without moving forward, keeping the hind legs on the ground without moving them, so that he does not keep time with his hind legs, as in all the other airs. This lesson is used to prepare a horse for leaping with greater freedom, and to gain control of his forehand . . .

Courbette. This is a leap in which the horse goes up higher in front, a sustained and heightened version of the Mézair, in which the hind legs go forward with a low but smart action, in concert with the forelegs at the moment when they come to the ground.

Croupade. This is a higher leap than the Courbette, both in front and behind, in which, while the horse is in the air, he gathers up his hind feet and legs under him, keeping them at the same height as the forefeet.

Balotade. This is a leap in which, while all four feet are in the air, at an equal height, the horse flexes the hind pasterns so as to show the soles of his feet, as if to kick (without actually doing so, as in the capriole) instead of folding his hind legs under him, as in the croupade.

Capriole. This is the highest and most perfect of all leaps. While the horse is in the air, and level from front to rear, he launches a kick as if, as it were, to tear himself in two, so that his hind legs shoot out like arrows; formerly this air was called "knotting the aiguillette" (or, tying the shoulder-knot).

The Step and Leap. This consists of three actions: first, a shortened gallop or terre-à-terre; second, a courbette; and the third, a capriole, and so on, over again. Horses which do not feel strong enough to repeat the capriole do this of their own volition and even the strongest leapers, when they are beginning to wear out, do it to relieve the strain and to give themselves more time for the leap.

Pages 96–97
ALBINO STALLION

The albino is not a breed but rather a color type born white with blue eyes. Genuine albinos with no color pigment at all and pinkish red skin and red eyes occur in most animal species, but 191 they do not exist in horses. Because the iris is light, the black of the pupil stands out, which gives this type of horse a completely different expression from that of dark-eyed equines. In this photograph the animal's halter and heavy head and thick neck conjure up images of a time when no important military battle could have been won without horses.

Probably one of the greatest horse societies of all time was that of the Mongols. Monique and Hans D. Dossenbach tell of the people of Genghis Khan:

Without the horse most of their battles and campaigns of conquest would have been unimaginable. Never before had the horse played such a central role, except perhaps in the lives of the Huns. There was no infantry in the Mongolian army; every soldier was a horseman. During the campaigns the Mongols' horses also provided the greater part of the men's rations. They milked the mares and let the milk thicken to a sour curd cheese in leather skins, to be eaten later just as it was or thinned with milk and drunk. Small amounts of blood were regularly taken from the horses in much the same way as the Masai herdsmen now living in East Africa extract blood from the zebus. Finally the horses were slaughtered for their meat . . .

This method of obtaining food and their custom of frequently changing horses meant that they required a great many riding animals. It is said that each soldier possessed eighteen or twenty horses. At times the Mongolian army consisted of over 200,000 soldiers and an estimated four or five million horses.

Pages 98–99
PERCHERON

The Percheron originated from Le Perche, a region south of Normandy. In spite of its large size and power it is endowed with elegant and graceful action, which makes it ideal for use as a vaulting horse.

Of all present-day equestrian activity, not only is vaulting one of the most beautiful to watch, but the spectator is given the chance to witness human and horses engaged in an activity that can be traced back to Roman times. I would imagine that the Greeks and people of Crete may have also participated in this near-ballet with equines. Anyone who loves horses, gymnastics, and dance will be delighted with vaulting.

My friend and authority on the subject, Elizabeth Searle writes:

Vaulting, gymnastics on the back of the moving horse began with the Romans as part of their basic riding instruction. In Medieval Europe it was also used in training knights in the art of horsemanship. Gradually the exercises became stylized and were practiced in the gymnasium instead of on the live horse. This type of vaulting, using the leather side of the "horse," is still a part of international competitive gymnastics. Another outgrowth of the original vaulting on a living horse found its way into the circus, where it is still a popular attraction. Modern cavalries also used vaulting on the moving horse as a foundation for riding; in fact, a vaulting competition among cavalry teams was introduced into the Olympic Games held in Antwerp in 1920.

Page 100
PERCHERON

In this photograph, the vaulter has sprung from the back of the cantering horse to soar into the sky before returning to earth.

Upon seeing vaulting for the first time, one immediately thinks of the bull-dancers of Crete in which man and bull appeared publicly together in a spectacle charged with danger, grace, and dexterity. Though the bull was important as a religious figure to many early civilizations—and remains so today—the Greeks were the first people to deify the horse. Monique Dossenbach writes:

. . . the horse played a much greater role in the cultural life of the Greeks than it had in any other earlier civilization. Its privileged position is reflected in the many ways it is depicted, both in art and in myth. The Sun god Helios in his four-horsed chariot rises up in the eastern sky; Eos goddess of the Dawn, is pulled from there by the two horses, Lampos and Phaeton; horses are harnessed to the chariot of her sister, the Moon goddess Selene; Pegasus, the winged horse, drags around lightning and thunder belonging to the all-powerful god Zeus; the chariot of Ares, the god of War, is driven by his sons Phobos (Terror) and Deimos (Fear); Pluto uses a horse-drawn chariot to carry Persephone off to Haeles; and when Hercales takes the town of Eles he rides the immortal stallion, Arion, the son of Poseidon.

Pages 102–103
SOMALI WILD-ASS FOAL

The first time I saw a Somali wild ass, it seemed that the creatures before me more resembled delicate characters from a Disney film rather than the inhabitants of some of Africa's harshest terrain. Though it was near evening and the sky had been warming up the colors of the landscape around us, still the subtle natural lavender then almost rose-pink of the animals' coats made them some of the most lovely equines I had ever seen. The Somalis' soft fur colors were emphasized by their black-mascaraed eyes and the black fur that fringed their ears and exquisitely striped their legs. There was something magically ancient about them, as though seconds before they might have stepped out of some stylized Egyptian frieze.

The Somali wild ass is among the rarest of the world's equines. In captivity they number little more than fifty—only one has ever been born in the Western Hemisphere, and in the wild a mere five hundred are estimated to still survive.

Pages 104–107
SPANISH STALLIONS

At the time of Goya and until the last part of the nineteenth century, horses in southern Spain wore brightly colored trappings such as those on these two Andalusian stallions. When Bizet wrote *Carmen*, his Don José and the gypsy gang of bandits that he joined certainly would have adorned their horses with these bridles, which are still made in the town of Ronda that is mentioned by Mérimée in his short novel.

Though white or gray are the colors most identified with Andalusians, they also come in bay and black. Even in 1845, noted travel writer Richard Ford wrote about these horses:

> That of Andalucia takes precedence of all; he fetches the highest price, and the Spaniards in general value no other breed; they consider his configuration and qualities as perfect, and in some respects they are right, for no horse is more elegant or easy in his motions, none are more gentle or docile, none are more quick in acquiring showy accomplishments, or in performing feats of a styling agility; he has very little in common with the English blood-horse; his mane is soft and silky, and is frequently plaited with gay ribbons; his tail is of great length . . . it often trails to the very ground, while the animal has perfect command over it, lashing it on every side as a gentleman switches his cane; therefore, when on a journey, it is usual to double tie it up, after the ancient pig-tails of our sailors.

Page 109
SPANISH WALK

To watch a horse worked well on the long reins (or in hand) is to witness controlled beauty in which man and animal at times practically attain oneness. Though horses were domesticated sometime between 3000 and 2000 B.C., it was not for another five hundred years that evidence shows equus to have been reined and bridled. Monique Dossenbach writes:

> From this time on, the horse was to play an increasingly important role. Soon it began to appear in reliefs and paintings, these drawings indicating that to the Egyptians the horse had become one of the novelest of animals.
>
> As yet no form of bridle or headstall was used. When horses were harnessed in front of the chariots, a kind of frill was put around the middle of their neck and reins fastened to it, which when pulled, increased the pressure on the animal's

neck and made it slow or stop. This method was commonly used for controlling Asiatic wild asses. It has been suggested that the Hyksos used a simple bit made of a straight piece of metal, but this seems very unlikely, for if they had possessed such a device the Egyptians would certainly have adopted it. The early Egyptian charioteers first used a bridle with a low slung noseband. This pressed on the cartilage of the animal's nose and restricted its ability to breathe; not a particularly refined method but very effective.

Pages 110–111
LUSITANO STALLION

The respective ages of stallion and youth in this image are probably roughly those of Alexander and Bucephalus at the time of their first encounter. Of the many legends and stories of this association, perhaps the most delightful centers on a portrait that was painted of the famous pair by a celebrated artist called Apples. When the portrait was finished it was taken to Alexander who did not seem at all pleased with the painting. Bucephalus, however, who was also present, neighed in recognition when he saw the extremely life-like equine staring back at him. Apples then turned to Alexander and said: "Your majesty's horse is a better judge of painting than is his noble master."

The black Portuguese stallion in this photograph has the same slightly Roman nose and heavy-boned impressive head that we imagine Bucephalus to have had. Unclear are the origins of the Lusitano, though they are probably very similar to the Andalusian with which it shares some characteristics. Though it does not possess the dream-like beauty of the Andalusian, the Portuguese horse is more athletic, which makes it ideal for use by the rejoneador in the Portuguese bullfight. The tourist who finds himself in Portugal during the summer should not miss a corrida, especially if he or she has the opportunity to see it in Lisbon's Campo Pequeno ring. Sitting in this pictorial structure while watching the rejoneadors in their period dress mounted on magnificent, highly trained Lusitano stallions, makes one feel more part of a medieval dream than of the reality of twentieth-century Portugal.

Pages 112–113
WOMAN AND ARAB STALLION

Since the beginning of time beautiful women and horses have been the romantic protagonists of myths and legends. Perhaps one of the most interesting of these is a Mongolian legend that explains the birth of Torgut, marking the creation of the human and animal kingdoms. The heroine of the legend is Irgit, a well-born young wife of the leader Oerlik, a man who was unable to give his wife children. One day when Irgit is out with her shepherdess, they meet "three shining women with wings" who tell them, "We know how sad you are that you have no son. Go early tomorrow morning to the Lake called Ulan-or. There you will see a strong and spirited animal, a deer without horns. Go up to it. You will have a son."

José Anton Benton relates the rest of his story:

The next day the air was warm and Irgit asked Oerlik if she should not go to the Lake Ulan-or? Oerlik lay in his tent on his cushions, with his hounds all around him. She said: "I wish you would get up." Oerlik replied: "But I am very comfortable here."

So she went slowly over the hills to the lake and called through her cupped hands, "Oh, where are you, deer without horns?" Perhaps it would not come after all. But on the other side of the marsh, from a clump of birches she heard a loud whinny. The ground thundered and the stones shot fire under the powerful hooves as a magnificent stallion appeared—the leader Tarpan. His head was like that of a pike, the neck muscled under the shiny coat. His eyes blazed but were unafraid. As soon as he perceived Irgit he stopped short, threw up his head and reared. His lips were open and he showed his teeth—he had forty. From his nostrils there came forth vapour . . .

The plains were alight and flashes of fire illuminated the air like drops of water falling from an oar. A whiff of mist came up from the lake and seemed to cover the gleaming plain, and then Irgit, and then the spirited animal.

When the mist cleared, she was sitting on the stallion's back, like an amazon gently carried.

Irgit's son was called Torgut. On the day of his birth there came from the North an endless procession of horses, stallions, mares and foals—all Tarpan's folk and he at their head. They joined Oerlik's tribe and paid him homage. Thus the human and the animal kingdom was created.

Pages 114–115
APPALOOSA HORSES

The Nez Percés Indians are responsible for the development of the Appaloosa, which takes its name from the Palouse river that crossed the Indians' territory. Through careful, selective breeding they perfected the spotted patterns on the coats of their animals. There are many variations on the six basic spot patterns: frost, leopard, marble, snowflake, spotted blanket, and white blanket. Spotted horses are also found in Chinese art of the T'ang dynasty (A.D. 618–907), in Egyptian and Persian art, and even in the cave dwellings at Pech Merle which were done in the Upper Paleolithic period.

As strikingly marked as were their horses, the American Indians further decorated them with natural materials and paint to make this chapter in equine-human relationships one of the most colorful of all. The painting of horses by the Indians is doubly fascinating for they did not do so for the mere sake of adornment, but because all of the designs they painted on their animals were of profound and significant meaning. These markings were symbols of past conquests, invocations for good fortune, and medicine to enhance a horse's natural abilities. While each tribe had individual symbols with only meaning to its people, there were also basic symbols and decorations that were familiar and used by all tribes.

The most basic of the painted symbols and decorations were the following: circles were thought to increase the animal's ability to see and smell danger; stripes recounted war honors; dots evoked a prayer that hail would fall on the enemy; a palm print signified vengeance against the rider's foes; thunder stripes were used to honor the god of offensive war; arrows painted on hoofs were thought to make a horse run faster; a second palm print sym-

bolized a mission accomplished; U-shaped markings signified the number of horses captured; a long wavy line with a circle at one end was the medicine symbol for the snake; decorative feathers on the head and tail signified past victories; and leaves were a reminder of wounds (the actual injury itself was marked by a circle and dots).

Pages 116–117
INDIAN HORSES

The American Indians painted and decorated their horses to a far greater degree than is shown in most western films and graphic art. The colors they used were strong and the designs bold so that the already dramatic combination of man and horse was made even more striking when so painted.

Paint was derived from a variety of animal, vegetable, and mineral sources. Bull berries and the moss on pine trees, for example, provided yellow, as did Buffalo gallstone. Duck manure was used to produce blue. Crimson-colored earth and crushed reddish-yellow rocks were used to produce red. Thomas E. Mails, author of *Mystic Warriors of the Plains*, tells us that:

> A warrior often painted his favorite war horse with the same pattern and colors he used for his own face and body. And when he was preparing for ceremonial events for journeys into enemy territory, he painted his horse at the same time he painted himself. The main thing to bear in mind is that a painted horse always carried a message about his owner, hence sometimes the quality of the horse bearing the marks—although a painted horse might not always be the one the owner had ridden on the raids described.

> The total effect of a painted warrior and horse upon those who saw them was often stunning, and many Indian accounts mention the striking impression they made. One aged Crow warrior still carried the picture of a Sioux rider he had encountered a half century before, whose entire body and horse were covered with bright blue paint and white dots.

Undoubtedly the most dramatic of all the airs above the ground is the capriole as performed here mounted on an Andalusian stallion. It has been speculated that this maneuver was devised during the Middle Ages by mounted soldiers to scatter and injure the enemy when fighting in close quarters. Crowded about by battling foot soldiers, the horse suddenly springs into the air, thrusting forward and extending its front legs while kicking out with its hind legs to knock aside the enemy.

Of all breeds of horses, the Arabian and the Andalusian for pure beauty are more the favorites of artists than are other horses. True graphic representations of Thoroughbreds are many, but in those paintings and engravings, the sport of racing is part of the attraction. However, with the Arabian and the Andalusian, the attraction is sheer physical beauty of the animal itself.

When one looks at the picture of this Arabian mare the aesthetics of her physique immediately charm the viewer; the large limpid eye; the thin skin that makes more prominent her veins and bones; the refinement of her head and her long, graceful neck; the large nostrils and small ears. Legend tells us that such a mare was one of five selected by Mohammed to mother all future generations of Arabian horses. Donald Braider, author of *The Life, History, and Magic of the Horse*, writes:

The chronicles of Mohammed tell us that the prophet maintained a large herd of trained horses. He subjected them to the following test: About one hundred animals were deprived of water for three full days and then were freed from the enclosure where they had been confined. All naturally rushed toward the nearest watering place but hardly had Mohammed released them when he ordered the horns of battle to be blown. Wild with thrust, almost all the mares continued galloping toward water and paid no attention to the summons. But five came abruptly to a halt and dutifully responded to the prophet's call, trotting back to his side. Having proved themselves to be totally obedient, this little group of mares was singled out for Mohammed's blessing. They were well-known thereafter as "the five mares of the Prophet," and became the most cherished dams of Islam. (By contrast, Mohammed is known to have shown special favor to only one stallion, named Borak.) The mares foaled the finest of all Arab stock, and from the group derived the only strain of Arab horses that could legitimately carry the name of *asil*—animals of pure blood.

Whatever truth lies behind these accounts, it is indisputable that the Bedouin herdsmen, who often hired themselves out as cavalrymen to whatever princeling offered the highest proportion of booty, bred for this purpose horses of uncommon beauty, stamina and speed. It is equally plain that the spread of Islam was accomplished on horseback. For this reason, Mohammedanism was disseminated much more rapidly than Christianity.

Horses of North Africa, the Libyan, or Barb, probably traces its origin to the Numidian horse which was crossed with the Oriental horse during the numerous invasions of North Africa, the first of which took place in A.D. 700.

The horse's place in romantic adventure is without parallel. Images such as the one on this page of women being swept away by their heroes on the backs of stallions have long been popular ones.

Animals in general were so significant to the Egyptians that they made many of them into their gods. The importance of the horse in their culture may be verified by the surviving paintings and pieces of equine sculpture that were found in or near the pyramids.

Pages 126–127
MARE AND FOAL

This Mediterranean field and its inhabitants might have captured the eye and canvas of Manet as horses have captivated artists since the beginning of time. No other animal has so frequently been drawn, painted, and sculpted, as have been equines. Although some painters who used horses in their work did not feel comfortable drawing them, Édouard Manet, unlike Delacroix and Géricault, who knew how to depict horses accurately, had to base his animals on British sporting prints. "Not being in the habit of painting horses," he explained to his friend Berthe Morisot, "I copied mine from those who knew best how to do them."

The list is long of those artists who immortalized equines and who in turn were immortalized by the horses they painted and sculpted. In fact, upon viewing it, one wonders, what painter wasn't captivated by equines: Leonardo da Vinci, Dürer, Raphael, Michelangelo, Titian, Van Dyck, El Greco, Rubens, Rembrandt, Velázquez, Goya, Stubbs, Delacroix, Géricault, Degas, Pissaro, Renoir, Toulouse-Lautrec, Gauguin, Munch, Dufy, Chagall, and Picasso.

Acknowledgments.

Many people in different parts of the world contributed to the creation of this book. Without their generosity, expertise, and love of horses it could not have been completed.

My deepest thanks go to that marvelous horseman Alvaro Domecq Romero and the Andalusian School of Equestrine Art of Jerez de la Frontera for the long hours—daybreaks to dusks—during which they displayed their skill and beauty before my cameras. In Spain good friends Paco Lazo, Antonio Romero, Juan Manuel Urquijo, and Miguel Angel Cardenas also contributed their time or their lovely mares and stallions. Special thanks in that country also goes to Jose Franco and Kitty Witwer.

In America Joan Embery and her husband, Duane Pillsbury, proved their great love for horses and friendship by again and again offering their valuable support and knowledge. Deepest thanks also go to The Most Reverend and Mrs. Robert Q. Kennaugh, Debra Walter, Linda Bishop, and Julie Lang. Other friends whose contribution of time or horses was indispensable to the making of this book were Ann Heber, Valerie Escalera, Vivienne Lundquist, William Shatner, Elizabeth Searle, Jeff Moore, Joyce Post, Inez Fort, Ken Childs, Linda Flick, Linda Thompson, Patty Saccoman, Dick Broün, Sally Bowlby, Victoria Dubiel, Sherrye and Jim Scherkenback, Gale, Julie, Zay, and Jody Ebson, Bill Notley, Mary and Mimi Page, Betty Moe, Ernie Eaton, Tracy Viser, Mark Vavra, Clark Mires, Will White, John Dixon, David Kader, Don Rowan, Scott Francis, Eddie Marquez, Rudolf Geissmann, and Mary Daniels.

Throughout the years I have counted on the friendship and support of Budd and Mary Boetticher, whose valuable assistance will always be appreciated as it is with this book.

At the San Diego Wild Animal Park I have had the good fortune to benefit from the best of men and friends, Rich Massena, along with the help of Jim Dolan, Larry Killmar, Jeff Fuller, and Joe Shuler. At the San Diego Zoo, I thank Georgeanne Irvine, Boo Shaw, and Chris Petersen.

Ron Henriques and Alden Townsend were of help time after time as were Gary Stadler and his wife, Lori, who I thank for a special good spell placed on this effort. For his continued friendship and assistance over the years, I thank Joe Saccoman.

In Mexico, for their interest in this project I express my deepest thanks to Marcela and Raúl Martinez. For his concern there I also thank Antonio Ariza and the Casa Domecq.

John Fulton has my gratitude for the excellent drawings that illustrate these pages.

Elias García and his staff I thank for making the color separations, along with Jerry Dean and Mike Euriell of Chromacolor for developing my film.

My good friend José Lopez has my deepest gratitude for keeping my cameras operating, as does Nancy Ridley for the typing of this manuscript.

In England I thank my friend Marilyn Tennent, as well as Sonia and Charles Windsor, Colleen Borcik, Audrey and Judith Butcher, George

Tickner, and Max and Joan Diamond and the British Jousting Association.

It would be unfair to not once more mention Rick Fabares for the creative effort and long hours in the lab that he put into each of these pictures.

My deepest thanks also go to Charlie Jackson and Mesa Photo, into whose hands each of my transparencies was placed to create the artistic effect for which I was searching.

For their continued support and encouragement I also thank my agent, Gloria Loomis, and, at William Morrow, Larry Hughes, Sherry Arden, Al Marchioni, and Lela Rolontz.

Barbara Chance, who did the delightful drawings for *Unicorns I Have Known*, was again with me while the layout was done for this book, and I thank her for her friendship and good advice.

To all of the other persons who helped with shoots but who are not mentioned here, I give my heartfelt thanks.

For taking care of me during my stay in America, I thank my mother and my brother, Ron, and sister-in-law, Gale.

Grateful acknowledgement is made for permission to quote material from the following words: *Centennial*, by James Michener, copyright © 1974 by Marjay Production Inc.; reprinted by permission of Random House, Inc. *Fire From Heaven*, by Mary Renault, copyright © 1969 by Mary Renault and *Persian Boy*, by Mary Renault, copyright © 1972 by Mary Renault; both reprinted by permission of Pantheon Books, a Division of Random House, Inc. and the Estate of Mary Renault.

Lastly, I thank James A. Michener, who for twenty-five years has been my inspiration and my friend. To him I owe a debt that can never be repaid.